# THE ORIGINS OF CONSCIOUSNESS

*The Origins of Consciousness* challenges the dominant view that consciousness is an emergent property of the complex human brain.

Based on his pioneering research on a variety of organisms, Vallortigara argues that the most basic forms of mental life do not require large brains, and that the neurological surplus observed in some animals such as humans is likely at the service of memory storage, not of the processes of thought or, even less, of consciousness. The book argues for a simple neural mechanism that can provide the crucial event that brings into effect the minimum condition for subjective experience. Implications of the hypothesis for the appearance of consciousness in different organisms are discussed, as well as links with a variety of fascinating human phenomena such as disorders of consciousness, tickling and visual illusions.

Challenging widely accepted theories of consciousness, the book is a must-read for students and researchers of human and animal consciousness.

**Giorgio Vallortigara** is Professor of Neuroscience and Animal Cognition at the University of Trento, Italy. He previously taught at the University of Trieste and was Adjunct Professor at the School of Biological, Biomedical and Molecular Sciences at the University of New England in Australia.

# THE ORIGINS OF CONSCIOUSNESS

## Thoughts of the Crooked-Headed Fly

*Giorgio Vallortigara*

Routledge
Taylor & Francis Group

LONDON AND NEW YORK

Designed cover image: LAGUNA DESIGN/SCIENCE PHOTO
LIBRARY via Getty Images

First published in English 2025
by Routledge
4 Park Square, Milton Park, Abingdon, Oxon OX14 4RN

and by Routledge
605 Third Avenue, New York, NY 10158

*Routledge is an imprint of the Taylor & Francis Group, an informa business*

Translated by Bennett Bazalgette-Staples

Published in Italian by Adelphi Edizioni 2021

*British Library Cataloguing-in-Publication Data*
A catalogue record for this book is available from the British Library

*Library of Congress Cataloging-in-Publication Data*
Names: Vallortigara, Giorgio, 1959- author.
Title: The origins of consciousness : thoughts of the crooked-headed fly /
Giorgio Vallortigara.
Other titles: Pensieri della mosca con la testa storta. English
Description: Abingdon, Oxon ; New York, NY : Routledge, 2025. | Includes
bibliographical references and index. |
Identifiers: LCCN 2024015586 (print) | LCCN 2024015587 (ebook) |
ISBN 9781032792132 (hardback) | ISBN 9781032792125 (paperback) |
ISBN 9781003491033 (ebook)
Subjects: LCSH: Consciousness. | Psychology, Comparative.
Classification: LCC BF311 .V24413 2025 (print) | LCC BF311 (ebook) |
DDC 153--dc23/eng/20240520
LC record available at https://lccn.loc.gov/2024015586
LC ebook record available at https://lccn.loc.gov/2024015587

ISBN: 978-1-032-79213-2 (hbk)
ISBN: 978-1-032-79212-5 (pbk)
ISBN: 978-1-003-49103-3 (ebk)

DOI: 10.4324/9781003491033

Typeset in Sabon
by KnowledgeWorks Global Ltd.

# CONTENTS

# ACKNOWLEDGEMENTS

I owe Giuseppe Trautteur double thanks for his patience in reading and his friendly condescension for invading the field: the topics of cybernetics that are touched upon in this book are part of Giuseppe's scientific history, from the period when the likes of Norbert Wiener and Warren McCulloch "were at home in Naples".[1]

## Note

1 See http://www.cittadellascienza.it/centrostudi/2016/03/quando-heisenberg-e-wiener-erano-di-casa-a-napoli/.

# INTRODUCTION

I am sitting at a desk in the Institute of Entomology at the University of Padua. There is another guy sitting just near me. He looks up from the eyepiece of his microscope. "Psychology?" He casts his gaze back to the slide, but after a while he turns to me again, looking somewhat puzzled. "Antlions – I don't suppose they've really got enough psychology to be worth studying." I limit myself to smiling wryly by way of response.

The scene dates back almost 35 years. My mentor, a professor from Padua University in Animal and Comparative Psychology,[1] had referred me to one of his colleagues in Entomology so that I might learn more about the life of the species. At the time, I kept antlions in my room, inside slim plastic boxes resting on a sheet of paper, so the sound they made – a sort of pattering, produced by the sand kicked up by the animal as it fell on the paper – would wake me up if I happened to doze off during my long hours of observation (these little beasts are most active in the evening).

Going back even further in time, I might have been seven or eight when a playmate drew my attention to conical holes in the ground, visible in the finest soil in the garden, which showed up in clusters of five or six, spaced a few millimetres apart, the diameter of which varied from half a centimetre to three or four centimetres. My companion picked up an ant between his fingers and dropped it into one of the cones. The animal landed on the sand and immediately tried to climb back up, but the steep, crumbling walls made climbing difficult. From the bottom of the upturned cone, something began to move, throwing sand directly towards the ant, which fell back down into the top of the cone. The insect began to climb once more, but overwhelmed by a new clump of sand, it fell back to the bottom again, where it slowly began to sink. After a while, only the head and the front part of the thorax

DOI: 10.4324/9781003491033-1

with its little legs remained visible. The ant moved convulsively, sinking even further, until it disappeared completely: the antlion had caught it. I saw it re-emerge from the sand a few minutes later, no more than a chitin exoskeleton, motionless and drained of all its juices. With a sharp knock of its head, similar to that used previously for throwing sand, the antlion finally ejected the ant from its conical trap.

I studied antlions for a while, trying to understand what mechanisms the animals used in the construction of their conical holes, but without much success. Then, as happens at that time of life, my interests quickly turned to new topics.[2]

At the University of Sussex, where I continued my education, there was a colleague working on jumping spiders, in particular on the way these animals are able to get around obstacles by "keeping in mind" the prey that has disappeared from sight. I had investigated the same "detour" behaviour in chicks of the domestic fowl, so we kicked a few ideas around. Another researcher was studying memory in Hermissenda, a snail similar to Aplysia, the marine gastropod made famous by Eric Kandel's Nobel Prize-winning studies. But none of these beasts aroused my attention in particular. For a long time, I had no other intellectual exchanges with insects or other invertebrates – "small neuron systems" in neurobiologist jargon.

In 2008, I spent a sabbatical in Australia with my friend and long-time collaborator Lesley Rogers from the University of New England. With Lesley, I had been exploring the mechanisms and evolutionary origins of brain asymmetry for many years. We had recently received news of a remarkable result obtained by Mandyam Srinivasan (Srini)'s laboratory at the Australian National University in Canberra: bees trained to associate an odour with a sugar reward with only the right antenna learned the task faster than bees trained with only the left antenna. Were the bees' brains perhaps asymmetrical, like those of humans and other vertebrates?[3] We spent a while in Srini's lab and then we got down to work, repeating and expanding the experiments. Inexperienced as we were, we ran into a few mishaps. Like when we were attacked by the insects while hunting for a hive of indigenous bees that had been reported to us in the old, abandoned building of the physiology department. The hive was on the outside wall, near the frame of a window. We were trying to collect some specimens, when suddenly the buzzing sound of the bees changed in pitch. Lesley was just in time to beat a hasty retreat and shout at me to close the window and make a run for it. We rushed inside, where lab benches and outdated equipment were piled up. Unfortunately, a couple of bees had got tangled in Lesley's hair. The walls of the building thus resounded to the sound of crushing slaps landing amid the greying locks of a prestigious member of the Australian Academy of Sciences.

Back in Italy, after a few years in Trieste, I accepted a new position at the University of Trento, and I was there waiting for work to be completed on my new, irredentist laboratory.[4]

According to current European Union legislation,[5] invertebrates such as insects are not animals. In order to conduct experiments on fish, amphibians, mammals and birds (note the order, which reflects my personal view of the pinnacle of "creation"), it is necessary for the university or research centre to be equipped with a standardised enclosure, and all experiments must be screened, supervised and approved by various committees; first, internal to the university and then, ministerial. This does not apply in the case of bees, cockroaches, lice and the like. As I said, they are not even animals according to current legislation, and often also according to common thought. So, in order not to remain idle, I decided to return to my old interest in simple brains, continuing my research into the asymmetry of the bee's nervous system. In my plans, this was to be a stopgap solution, a temporary activity while waiting to return to my firm favourites: farmyard hen chicks. But the study of brain asymmetry progressively grew to involve other projects as well as outstanding young scientists; so today my laboratory hosts not only some of the traditional guests of neuroscience research institutes – mice, rats, chicks and zebrafish (listed in random order) – but also a considerable number of bees, bumblebees and fruit flies. Not quite antlions but at least some of their distant relatives... Every now and then, in fine weather, I can't resist the temptation and take an antlion home or to my office. I leave it there just to keep me company. I like to hear the crackle of sand falling on paper, my auditory madeleine, and thus recognise the sound of an old friend.

As a scholar of nervous systems and their products – minds – I am interested in the general lessons that can be drawn from the study of these miniaturised brains.[6] A bee has 960,000 neurons in its encephalic ganglion. With these neurons alone, it is able to perform cognitive feats which I will describe in detail in this book, such as learning to discriminate paintings by Monet from paintings by Picasso, and then recognising new specimens of Monet and Picasso paintings, ones previously unseen. With its 960,000 neurons, the bee can distinguish different human faces, identifying them even when they are shown rotated to a different angle. Again, the bee can abstractly categorise stimuli as "the same" or "different", regardless of the nature and characteristics of the stimuli.

Humans certainly defend themselves respectfully when compared with bees or other creatures with miniature nervous systems. We too can recognise faces, classify a painting as a Picasso or a Monet and recognise things as being the same or different. But the human brain has 86 billion neurons: the real mystery is not how it can recognise faces or Monet's paintings, but just what it does with all the rest of those neurons.

I have come to believe that by studying the miniature brains of creatures like bees or flies, we should be able to enucleate the basic operating principles of minds. Those are the "primary principles" which our disciplines still seem to lack, and from which everything else should logically descend, including the nature and evolutionary origin of conscious experience.

The baseline conditions for the appearance in the world of creatures who have *experience* of the world can only be established by going back to the dawn of minds, to the first nervous systems to inhabit the planet.

I have tried to explore all this in the pages you are about to read, using mini-brains as a pretext, because – as you may have guessed – there may be some interesting links to be made between the antlion's brain and human psychology.

## Notes

1 Mario Zanforlin, who, together with Danilo Mainardi in Parma, Floriano Papi in Pisa and Leo Pardi in Florence, was among the forefathers of ethological studies in Italy. See E. Alleva (2009), "Storia dell'etologia italiana", in *La Cultura Italiana, Vol. VIII, Scienze e Tecnologie*, UTET, Turin.

2 For anyone curious about the strange vicissitudes that make up the life of a researcher, see Q&A Giorgio Vallortigara, *Current Biology* (2019), 29, R603–R622. https://www.sciencedirect.com/science/article/pii/S0960982219306086.

3 Vertebrates have a backbone, while invertebrates do not. The former are part of the group of the "chordates", animals characterised by the presence of a notochord, which is developed through the formation of a spinal column.

4 The laboratory is situated in Rovereto, the most irredentist town in Trentino. Edmondo Berselli, who lived in Rovereto until his first year of high school (without however betraying it as I did, for after having spent my childhood there, I did not return for 35 years), describes its essence thus: "it is with the echoes of the presence of Montaigne and Cagliostro in the secret parts of Via Mercerie and Vicolo Basadonna, and the certified memory (including the menu of the great lunch) of Christmas 1769 with the European event of the teenage Mozart concert that Rovereto is so magical" (Ewa-Mari Johansson, Massimo Mastrorillo [2008], *Attraverso Rovereto*, text by Edmondo Berselli and Emanuela Egon, Zandonai Editore, Rovereto.

5 An exception is made for the octopus. My colleagues who study this marvellous creature will forgive me, but I find it disgraceful that it has been elevated to the protected and exclusive heaven of vertebrates, while leaving animals such as the bee or the fruit fly in limbo without any real scientific justification.

6 I always tell my students that the term "mind" should not be used as a noun, for – as evolutionary biologist Ernst Mayr argued for the word "life" – it is rather the substantiation of a process. Life and mind are processes, not substances. One should therefore say – should it not be a cause of confusion with its two other meanings – "to mind", meaning the concrete processing of the nervous system, abandoning the use of the noun "mind" altogether. Pending this unlikely lexical reform, consider with indulgence the purely conventional use of the word "mind" in this book, which is in any case to be understood as merely shorthand for "what the brain does".

# 1
# EARTHWORM CONSCIOUSNESS

*Mental faculties.* There is little to say on this matter. We have seen that worms are timid. It may be doubted whether they suffer as much pain when injured as they seem to express by their contortions.

Charles Darwin

There is a rich literature on animal cognition, which often extends to the issue of animal consciousness. Much of the discussion is based on an argumentative style that information theorist Giuseppe Trautteur described as "the simple assertion that since animals appear to us to be conscious, therefore they are conscious" (personal communication).

Here by "consciousness" I mean the fact of having experience, i.e. that one *senses*, one *feels* something when one touches a cheek with one's fingers, smells peppermint or looks at the bottom of a scorched pot... And the confusion is caused by freely mixing up the subject of having experience with that of exhibiting certain behaviours. It is not obvious when and why certain behaviours, whether simple or complex, are accompanied by a *feeling* due to the fact of having experiences.

There are two arguments in today's thinking about consciousness that I particularly dislike, although they are widely accepted among my colleagues. The first relates to the existence of gradualism in experience, and therefore to the hypothesis that other animals may indeed be conscious, but *only a little.* What is "a little" supposed to mean? Either an organism is capable of experience or it is not. There is no halfway experience or piecemeal experience. Introspection is often invoked to support the gradualness of consciousness. Certainly, as soon as we are awake, or when we are about to fall asleep,

DOI: 10.4324/9781003491033-2

or when we have taken certain substances, our awareness of various aspects of the environment may be altered, but this does not mean that it is absent or half present. To be confused or to experience twilight states of consciousness does not mean being only partially conscious – it means experiencing certain *types* of experiences, with different content from usual. Even not being sure of having felt something is a kind of feeling.

In the case of other species, the question is whether they possess experience, but even if that were the case, this would not imply that the contents are necessarily the same as our experiences. Indeed, the experiences of different species could be incommensurable. However, to say that they are ontologically distinct (as first-person experiences) is quite different from asserting that they are present in quantity or to a lesser degree. Either other species have experiences (*their* experiences) or they do not.

The second topic is important for the themes discussed in this book. According to many of my colleagues, consciousness, the fact of having experiences, of *feeling* something, is linked to the amount or richness of structuring of the elements of the nervous system. Often the two topics are combined. We have no difficulty recognising consciousness in elephants (obviously because they "seem" conscious to us, in Trautteur's sense), but we doubt that worms are conscious, because they possess too few neurons and connections between neurons. Too bad it is never explained to us why and how the complexity of a nervous system should at some point (or gradually?) lead to the appearance of experiences.

Is there a critical threshold of size and complexity of the nervous system beyond which one suddenly becomes conscious? Or, if it is a matter of degree, between the worm supposedly with zero consciousness and the human with maximum, what would the wombat's score be? And that of the capybara?

Over the course of this book, I shall develop ideas that are antithetical to this manner of conceiving the problem of conscious experience. First, I will try to show how the relationship between the complexity of mental life and the structure of the nervous system is unlike what is commonly held. In particular, I will argue the rather extreme thesis that the basic forms of mental life do not require large brains, and that the neurological surplus observed in some animals is probably at the service of memory stores, not the processing of thought or consciousness. To do this, as a rhetorical tool, I shall draw on various facts that have emerged from studies of the cognitive capacities of organisms with miniaturised brains, such as bees. I will then recount how, throughout natural history, brains have incorporated a few simple stratagems to solve specific problems, and how surprising consequences have arisen from these, which reverberate in the functioning of our present-day nervous systems. Finally, by loosely blending the description of these stratagems with a number of ideas about perception and sensation, plundered from ancient Scottish philosophers and modern scholars of an oxymoronic "blind sight", I will try to suggest something about the reasons for the appearance of organisms capable of experience.

At the end of the book, I regret to reveal, you will not find an explanation of what consciousness is, but only a number of hypotheses on the minimum – but in my opinion necessary – conditions for its appearance. After all, one has to start somewhere.

# 2

# ROBINSON, THE CATERPILLAR AND THE BUTTERFLY

> Thank you for reminding me of those poor *Tenebrio molitor*: who perhaps did not know why they always had to take the same fork in the road every day. Like us, in the end.
>
> From an email by Ruggero Pierantoni, October 2016

Valentino Braitenberg, a South Tyrolean neuroanatomist and cyberneticist, once told me about the sense of inferiority he would experience on meeting individuals with out-of-the-ordinary ingenuity. As examples, he cited Francis Crick, the discoverer of the double helix structure of DNA, but also his old school friend Paul Mayr, or Josef Rottensteiner, a farmer from the Ortnerhof in Soprabolzano… one may often feel incapable of certain levels of performance, but this is not necessarily a good criterion for judging their complexity. Reading *Robinson Crusoe* as a boy, I found myself thinking: "Well, I probably wouldn't know how to do all that: build a grinder's wheel with a rope and a wheel, make pottery and a clay pipe, make clothes and an umbrella out of the skins from hunting wild goats." On the other hand, I felt I was a fair match for the ship's mutineers and I thought I could easily make friends with Friday. Among Robinson's many activities that had nothing to do with human beings, the only one to which I was prepared to attribute any aptitude was catching a parrot to teach it to speak, which is an exquisitely social activity. Thus, when later in life I learnt of the "hypothesis of the social function of the intellect" formulated by the evolutionary psychologist Nicholas Humprey, I was thunderstruck.[1]

Despite their apparent complexity, Humphrey observed, the physical-technological problems faced by Robinson Crusoe are relatively simple; the

DOI: 10.4324/9781003491033-3

difficult problems are instead those arising from interaction with other human beings: for Robinson, troubles first appear along with Friday's footsteps.

We do not usually appreciate the complexity and difficulty of social problems, either when we pursue goals aimed at enhancing community wellbeing through altruism and cooperation, or when we set ourselves manipulative tasks, such as tactical deception. This is because we human beings come into the world well equipped to deal with the dilemmas that arise from the relational sphere. Even when we experience conflicts with our fellow human beings, it is easy for us to intuit their nature and try to resolve them, possibly to our own advantage. However, there is nothing simple about the way we might communicate with Friday or with other members of our species in general.

Humphrey shares with primatologist Alison Jolly[2] the parenthood of the idea that complex minds develop in social groups in which individuals must weave intricate webs of interpersonal relationships, as is the case among humans, but also, to some extent, among other creatures: mammals such as apes or birds such as crows. Humphrey and Jolly's idea paved the way for the notion of the so-called "theory of mind": the human capacity to represent the mental states of others, and the question of whether the rudiments of this capacity can be found in other species.

Imagine observing a person hiding an object before your friend's eyes, choosing between two drawers the one on the left. Your friend then leaves the room and, without being seen, the person removes the object from the left drawer and places it in the right. Where will your friend look for the object once he or she re-enters the room? In the left-hand drawer, of course. What *he or she* believes does not correspond to what *you* know. Whether this ability to attribute a (in this case, false) belief to other individuals is a distinctive trait of our species is a matter of debate. The most convincing clue that we may not be the only ones to attribute mental states to others comes from a study that made use of sophisticated *eye-tracking* procedures to precisely measure where chimpanzees, gorillas and orangutans look while observing episodes of the kind described above.[3] The results show that the animals direct their gaze to the left drawer, as if they expect the actor (your friend) to look in that position on the basis of possessing a false belief.

As far as we know, the social life of some of the species with miniature brains, such as bees, while sophisticated in its own way, is not characterised by a similar level of subtlety in interaction between conspecifics. Curiously, however, the idea of the social function of the intellect was originally formulated for these very animals.

The most dorsal portions of insects' brains are called mushroom bodies (*corpora peduncolata*). You can see them in Figure 2.1; you can guess from the morphology why they were called that (they look a little like the chanterelle mushrooms that may be picked in the woods in autumn).

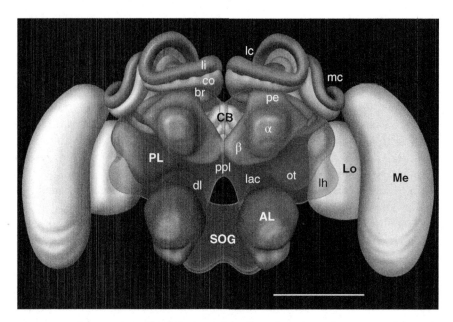

**FIGURE 2.1** Schematic representation of the bee's brain. At the top are the mushroom bodies. At the sides are the optic lobes (which process visual information), and at the bottom the antennal lobes (AL, which process olfactory information).

*Source:* Rybak, J., Kuss, A., Lamecker, H., Zachow, S., Hege, H., Lienhard, M., Singer, J., Neubert, K. and Menzel, R. (2010), "The digital bee brain: Integrating and managing neurons in a common 3D reference system". *Frontiers in Systems Neuroscience*, 4: 30.

These are "associative" nerve structures, i.e. ones where the information from the visual and olfactory sensory pathways converges. We know they play an important role in learning and memory. One piece of evidence comes from an attempt to provide an answer to a seemingly rather odd question.

Insects, as is well known, go through several stages in their development, prefiguring that of the adult insect: first they are larvae, then pupae and finally adult animals. ("What the caterpillar calls the end of the world, the rest of the world calls a butterfly," Lao Tze observes.) The antlions whose exploits had so impressed me were in fact antlion larvae. It is at the larval stage that the little animal performs the prodigious task of building cones in the sand, then hiding at the bottom, from where it can strike potential prey with well-aimed sand throws to make them fall in and thus catch them in its jaws (Figure 2.2).

As an adult, its appearance is indeed different, as is its behaviour. It somewhat resembles the dragonfly, and spends its short but intense life with the primary objective of mating, only to die shortly afterwards. But what happens to its memory when the insect changes during metamorphosis, transforming

**FIGURE 2.2**   a. The antlion larva; b. The adult insect; c. The antlion larva in its cone trap.

from larva to pupa and then from pupa to adult insect? What does an adult antlion remember, as it flutters in search of a mate, of the sandy cones it inhabited when a larva, or of the envelope in which it was cocooned when it was a pupa? Perhaps it has no memory of its pre-metamorphic stages, for in such stages it may not be able to learn and remember. But this seems implausible. Antlion larvae certainly do learn. For instance, it has been shown they can learn to associate a neutral stimulus with the onset of prey (this is known as "classical" or "Pavlovian" conditioning). If a brief vibratory stimulus repeatedly precedes the arrival of a prey in the trap cone, the animal will after a while begin to throw sand at the mere onset of the vibratory stimulus, even in the absence of the prey, i.e. anticipating its arrival.[4] The same does not occur, however, if the presentation of vibratory stimulus is not correlated with the arrival of food. However, it is possible for the insects to be unable to recall what they learnt in their larval past as adults, a bit like our own infantile amnesia: the still-mysterious phenomenon whereby we do not retain explicit memories of the very early years of our lives.

The problem was examined in an ingenious and little-known study published almost 40 years ago. The experiment was conducted in a two-armed maze using the larvae of the *Tenebrio molitor* beetle.[5] These animals show a distinct negative phototaxis, i.e. they shy away from light (as anyone who has turned on a torch in a dark room infested with cockroaches and observed their scuttling away knows). Every time the larva entered the wrong arm, a light was switched on as punishment, while if it entered the right one, the space remained dark. For half the animals, the right arm was the correct one; for the other half, the left. The larvae learnt the task. Then, once the animals had become adult insects, a sample drawn at random from the original population repeated the experiment, being allowed to choose, in the absence of punishment, whether to take the right or left arm at the fork. This experimental group was compared with a control group that in the larval stage had been through the maze the same number of times without any punishment whatsoever. The animals in the experimental group, which had been trained at the larval stage, maintained their learned choices, i.e. they continued to prefer the right arm, while the animals in the control group chose randomly between the two arms.

At the time the experiment was carried out, the hypothesis was that the neurons of the mushroom bodies, unlike the other neurons that are present at the larval stage and which are then replaced by others, pass through the various stages of metamorphosis unharmed, thus enabling the transfer of memories. More recent studies conducted on the fruit fly (*Drosophila melanogaster*) suggest that, at least as far as odour memories are concerned, three lobes of the mushroom bodies are involved: one of these (the gamma lobe) develops very early, while the other two (alpha and beta) develop just before the pupa stage. It may therefore be that only one portion of the mushroom bodies – the gamma lobe – survives the massive changes of metamorphosis, and that it is this portion that allows for the transit of memories.[6]

In 1850, zoologist Fèlix Dujardin (1801–1860) observed that the mushroom bodies, which he himself had first described, are much larger in social insect species than in solitary species. In his words:

> As intelligence dominates over instinct, the mushroom bodies and antennal lobes become larger than the total volume of the brain, as can be seen by comparing beetles, locusts, solitary wasps and, finally, social bees, where the mushroom bodies account for as much as one fifth of the brain and 1/940 of the whole body.
>
> (translated by Dujardin, 1850, p. 202)[7]

Although he is sometimes credited with leading the hypothesis that mushroom bodies are involved in memory and learning, this was not Dujardin's opinion. Gifted with an incredible talent as a microscopist, he fully described the structure of mushroom bodies, being especially fascinated by the region he called "les lobes à circonvolutions", to which the anatomist Edwin T.

Newton later assigned the name "calyces" (see Figure 2.1, median calyx and lateral calyx – mc and lc). Dujardin was struck by the folds and turns of the calyces, which reminded him of those in the human cerebral cortex, and by the fact that these folds were more pronounced in species such as bees and in social insects in general.[8] He was also interested in the control of voluntary action. He had noticed that certain insects, such as flies, which have tiny mushroom bodies, once decapitated continue for a while to display typical movements, not unlike those of intact animals, whereas insects such as bees, which possess highly developed mushroom bodies, almost completely cease all coordinated movements after decapitation. Dujardin's idea was that mushroom bodies provided animals with scope for intelligent behaviour and free will over purely instinctive actions.

Among the scholars who made a direct experimental contribution to confirming Dujardin's ideas was a person destined for greater fame in an entirely different sphere: the experimental psychologist Alfred Binet (1857–1911), the inventor of the first test on which the measurement of intelligence quotient was based.

Born in Nice and therefore, at the time, a citizen of the Kingdom of Sardinia, Alfredo Binetti moved to Paris when he was still young, where he first studied law, then medicine (but did not complete the course) and finally landed on the natural sciences. For his doctoral thesis, which he conducted on a species of beetles (from the family of Dytiscidae), he used techniques to ablate portions of the nervous tissue and observed how, after removal of the sub-oesophageal ganglion, the insects could maintain the coordinated movement of their limbs, whereas the same faculty vanished after removal of the supra-oesophageal ganglion (the brain proper).[9] At the same time, the physiologist Ernest Faivre showed how these insects can survive for months in the absence of the supra-oesophageal ganglion if fed by the experimenter, but are totally incapable of finding food on their own.[10] Faivre hypothesised an analogy between the encephalic trunk of mammals and the sub-oesophageal ganglion of insects, which are responsible for innate and stereotyped consumptive feeding behaviour. The supra-oesophageal ganglion, on the other hand, where the mushroom bodies are also located, would be crucial for the performance of the more complex aspects of food-seeking activity.

Thus, according to Dujardin, mushroom bodies were supposedly the seat of intelligence and sociality. This hypothesis has only been put to the test in recent years by reconstructing the phylogenetic tree and brain structure of a considerable number of hymenoptera species, the order of insects to which bees and wasps belong, along with their behavioural habits.

The insects at the base of the phylogenetic tree actually have small and structurally very simple mushroom bodies and, as was probably the case with their ancestors, the calyx region only receives olfactory, but not visual, afferents. Surprisingly, however, the appearance of large mushroom bodies, which receive and integrate both olfactory and visual information, is not observed with the appearance of sociality[11] but some 90 million years earlier.[12]

What kind of animals were these social insect ancestors already equipped with large mushroom bodies? They were parasitoids, akin to today's solitary wasps: insects that immobilise their prey with a venom, leaving them alive for consumption by their larvae. It seems that it was in order to achieve the type of behaviour that characterises life as parasitoids that the development of the insects' "cerebral cortex" – the mushroom bodies – became necessary.

The cognitive capacities of parasitoids were described by the great entomologist Jean-Henry Fabre (1823–1915),[13] who illustrated their complexities, especially when compared with the simple, wandering life of their ancestors who just laid their eggs on leaves.

The most famous case is that of the sand wasp (*Ammophila campestris*). Having captured a caterpillar or a grasshopper, the wasps immobilise their prey by injecting it with a poisonous substance. With neurosurgical expertise, the wasps proceed to make three successive injections, one for each ganglion in prey characterised by three separate ganglia, but with only one injection, localised in the encephalic ganglion, in prey where the ganglia are fused together.

The navigational skills and spatial memory of these wasps are remarkable. Having built a burrow in the sand, which will serve as a nest for the immobilised prey in which to lay the egg laid, the wasp makes reconnaissance flights before hunting to learn the configuration of the landscape so that it can find the nest again. As it takes care of several nests at once, the wasp will have to remember which nests already contain an egg with its corresponding meal (the larva that has emerged from the egg will in fact feed on the immobilised prey) and which ones are still empty. The choice of prey also requires careful evaluation and learning: young females on their first flights mainly use innate memories of the smell of their prey, but later learn visual characteristics such as colour and shape. The prey itself may be more or less profitable and, in the areas where it is caught, may be present in different densities, and all this is learnt by the predatory wasps.

In short, the intellectual challenges that have shaped the nervous systems of these animals are those of finding convenient prey for their larvae and spatial orientation for their return to the nests where they will lay their eggs. Social species such as bees, however, face the same problems: they must recognise and assess food sources – which for them are flowers rather than other insects – on an olfactory and visual basis, and they must orient themselves in the environment to return to the hive. It is feasible, therefore, that the adaptations to the social life of bees developed using the neural endowments that these animals *already had* at their disposal: endowments that had evolved almost 100 million years earlier, with the advent of parasitoids. Let us try to consider some of these social abilities in order to better understand their nature.

## Notes

1  N. Humphrey (1976), "The social function of intellect", in P. P. G. Bateson and R. A. Hinde (eds.), *Growing Points in Ethology*, chapter 9 (Cambridge: Cambridge University Press), 303–317.

2  A. Jolly (1966), "Lemur social behavior and primate intelligence". *Science*, 153: 501–506.

3  C. Krupenye, F. Kano, S. Hirata, J. Call and M. Tomasello, (2016), "Great apes anticipate that other individuals will act according to false beliefs". *Science*, 354: 110–114.

4  L. M. Guillette, K. L. Hollis and A. Markarian (2009), "Learning in a sedentary insect predator: Antlions (Neuroptera: Myrmeleontidae) anticipate a long wait". *Behavioural Processes*, 80: 224–232.

5  A. Borsellino, R. Pierantoni and B. Cavazza (1970), "Survival in adult mealworm beetles (*Tenebrio molitor*) of learning acquired at the larval stage". *Nature*, 225: 963–964. For recent studies on the topic of memory transfer during metamorphosis, see D. J. Blackiston, E. S. Casey and M. R. Weiss (2008), "Retention of memory through metamorphosis: Can a moth remember what it learned as a caterpillar?" *PLoS ONE*, 3(3): e1736. doi:10.1371/journal.pone.0001736; J. D. Armstrong, J. S. de Belle, Z. Wang and K. Kaiser (1998), "Metamorphosis of the mushroom bodies; large-scale rearrangements of the neural substrates for associative learning and memory in Drosophila". *Learning & Memory*, 5: 102–114; for a review see D. J. Blackiston, T. Shomrat and M. Levin (2015), "The stability of memories during brain remodeling: A perspective". *Communicative and Integrative Biology*, 27; 8(5): e1073424.

6  Incidentally, the analogy with infantile amnesia may not be peregrine. Infantile amnesia is observed in many species, e.g. it has been studied in rats, which do not remember as adults what they learned in the early stages after birth. Guinea pigs, on the other hand, which unlike rats are an early-developing (or *precocial*) species, show no infantile amnesia: what they learned and remember at a few days old they continue to remember as adults. High levels of neurogenesis in the hippocampus, such as can be observed in certain strains of mutant mice that have an alteration in a particular synaptic protein, are associated with higher rates of memory forgetting. One hypothesis that has been put forward is that childhood amnesia is related to neurogenesis phenomena. Traditionally, it was believed that in mammals the production of new neurons was completed at birth (except in special cases such as the olfactory bulb; in other taxonomic groups, such as birds, neurogenesis is known to occur in adulthood, for example in association with seasonal song learning). Instead, it has been discovered that the addition of new neurons continues even after birth, at least in the hippocampus, in a structure known as the dentate gyrus. The production of neurons peaks immediately after birth and then slowly declines. The ability to form stable memories would then go hand in hand with a decrease in the ability to generate new neurons. It may seem strange that the appearance of new neurons leads to a degradation of memories; one would expect the opposite. One has to consider, however, that this is a temporary effect, which depends on the age of the new neurons. As soon as they are born, new neurons begin to form connections by altering the existing connectivity, but once mature and stabilised in the network they will in turn participate in the storage of memories. For an in-depth discussion, see S. A. Josselyn and P. W. Frankland (2012), "Infantile amnesia: A neurogenic hypothesis". *Learning and Memory*, 19: 423–433.

7  F. Dujardin (1850), "Memoire sur le systéme nerveux des insects". *Annales des Sciences Naturelles* 14: 195–206.

8  Accurate information on Dujardin, along with much more on the arthropod brain, can be found in a wonderful book written by Nicholas J. Strausfeld (2012),

*Arthropod Brains. Evolution, Functional Elegance, and Historical Significance.* The Belknap Press of Harvard University Press, Cambridge, Mass.

9 The central nervous system of insects consists of a double chain of ganglia extending ventrally from the head to the abdomen, below the digestive canal (in vertebrates the nervous system is dorsal rather than ventral). Usually, one pair of ganglia can be observed for each body segment, but at the head there is a fusion of the first six pairs of ganglia into two distinct brain masses. One, the cerebrum (or brain), located immediately above the oesophagus, receives stimuli from the antennae and eyes; the other, the gnathocerebrum, is located below the oesophagus and innervates the appendages of the mouthparts. Binet's studies can be found in A. Binet (1894), "Contribution a l'étude du systèm nerveux sous-intestinal des insects" [Contribution to the study of the subintestinal nervous system of insects]. *Journal de l'Anatomie et de la Physiologie Normales et Pathologiques de l'Homme et des l'Animaux*, 30: 449–580.

10 E. Faivre (1857), "Du cerveau des Dytisques consideré dans se rapports avec la locomotion" [Of the brain of the Dytisci considered in its relationship with locomotion]. *Annales de Sciences Naturelles (Zoologie et Biologie Animale)*, sér. 4, 8: 245–274; E. Faivre (1864), "Reserches sur la distinction de la sensibilité et de l'excitabilité dans le diverse parties du system nervèux du Dytisque" [Research on the distinction of sensitivity and excitability in various parts of the nervous system of Dytiscus]. *Annales de Sciences Naturelles (Zoologie et Biologie Animale)*, sér. 5, 1:89.

11 Eusociality, with offspring care and the presence of castes is observed in Hymenoptera (bees, wasps and ants), Isoptera (termites) and Homoptera (aphids).

12 S. M. Farris and S. Schulmeister (2011), "Parasitoidism, not sociality, is associated with the evolution of elaborate mushroom bodies in the brains of hymenopteran insects". *Proceedings Royal Society of London B*, 278: 940–951. See also: L. Chittka, S. J. Rossiter, P. Skorupski and C. Fernando (2012), "What is comparable in comparative cognition?". *Philosophical Transactions of the Royal Society B*, 367: 2677–2685; M. D. Lihoreau, T. Latty and L. Chittka (2012), "An exploration of the social brain hypothesis in insects". *Frontiers in Physiology*, 442: 1–7; L. Chittka and P. Skorupski (2011), "Information processing in miniature brains". *Proceeding of the Royal Society of London B*, 278: 885–888.

13 J. H. Fabre (1879), *Souvenirs entomologiques: Premiere serie [Entomological souvenirs: Volumes 1–5]*. Paris: Librairie Ch. Delagrave.

# 3

# THE MOST INTERESTING SURFACE ON EARTH

> The surface of a human face is the most interesting surface on the Earth.
>
> Georg Lichtenberg

Faces attract our attention from birth, if not even before. In Figure 3.1 you can observe the electrical brain activity of infants as young as 64 hours old looking at two very similar stimuli, consisting of an oval with three dark discs inside. In the first stimulus, the discs are arranged canonically, like two eyes and a mouth; in the second, they are upside down.

As can be seen, the canonical face elicits a much more intense electroencephalographic response than the upside-down face.

There is no way to prevent an infant from seeing faces, no matter how precocious the age at which the experiment is conducted: a peek at the face of the midwife or mother, as soon as the newborn comes out, is no way to prevent it. Recently, however, this preference for facial configuration has even been observed in foetuses.[2] With a laser, two different configurations were projected onto the abdomen of pregnant women, consisting of discs bright enough to be perceived by the foetus. One configuration consisted of the three discs arranged in the usual "face" configuration, with two eyes at the top and a mouth at the bottom; in the other configuration, the arrangement of the discs was reversed in the up–down direction. The stimuli were presented at the edge of the foetus' visual field and were then moved laterally. Using an ultrasound scan system, it was observed that the foetus was more likely to turn its head when presented with the stimulus in the canonical face configuration than in that of the inverted face.

DOI: 10.4324/9781003491033-4

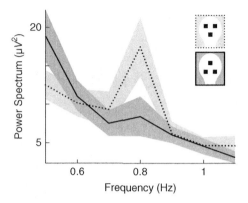

**FIGURE 3.1** Electroencephalographic response of 64-hour-old infants measured in the author's laboratory. The two types of stimuli were presented periodically, interspersed with visual noise, at a frequency of 8 Hz. One can see the greater response to the canonical face (dotted line) compared with the inverted face (solid line) in correspondence with the frequency of stimulus occurrence.

*Source:* Buiatti et al. (2018).[1]

A preference for these facial simulacra has been documented under controlled conditions in animals such as young rhesus macaques and domestic chicks, which had never seen any similar stimulus before (not even when in the womb or egg).[3]

Adult rhesus monkeys also look longer at images depicting faces or images that we humans tend to mistake for faces, such as those shown in Figure 3.2 (in the second column). This tendency to see faces in inanimate objects, or "pareidolia", has always been believed to reflect exquisitely cultural mechanisms unique to the human species, such as exposure to images that anthropomorphise inanimate objects, as occurs in cartoons or picture books. The fact that pareidolia may be observed in monkeys suggests instead that it has a biological basis.

Paying attention to faces from birth makes it possible to learn their characteristics more quickly, which is very important for animals such as monkeys, chickens or humans, who recognise each other individually and who, on the basis of this recognition, can predict the behaviour of different individuals – ones who might be aggressive, generous or a bully – and grasp the rank of each in the organisation of society (from the pecking order of chickens to the complex social structures of monkeys or humans).

It is therefore not surprising that in primates, sub-cortical structures have been described that direct the attention of infants towards stimuli resembling faces, as well as highly specific cortical areas devoted to the analysis of faces in adults, such as the so-called fusiform gyrus area. The, albeit cursory,

**FIGURE 3.2** Examples of conspecific faces (first column) and images of inanimate objects that in humans and monkeys are (second column) or are not (third column) perceived as faces.

*Source:* Taubert et al. (2017).[4]

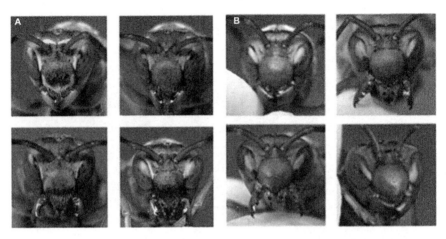

**FIGURE 3.3**  Examples of the facial configurations exhibited by different individuals of the species *P. fuscatus*.

*Source:* Tibbetts, Pandit and Nondorf (2018).[5]

activation of the same areas can already be seen in infants when they look at the configuration with the three inverted triangle discs.

Similar abilities to those of monkeys and humans have, however, also been described in paper wasps (*Polistes fuscatus*). These insects know how to recognise mates on the basis of the characteristics of their "faces", apparently using a mechanism dedicated to this precise function. A number of examples of the markings that make the faces of the wasps discernible from one another are shown in Figure 3.3.

Unlike foraging bees, which easily learn to discriminate between two stimuli in order to obtain a reward (such as a sugar-water solution), wasps, which can go weeks without feeding, learn more quickly when it comes to avoiding punishment. For this purpose, ethologist Elizabeth Tibbetts and her collaborators used a T-maze of which the floor was mildly electrified, except for the safe zone in one of the two arms in which the image of the correct stimulus was located.[6]

The wasps had to learn to discriminate between two stimuli. Each stimulus pair belonged to different categories. These might be, for example, the images of two different wasps, two different black-and-white geometric drawings, two caterpillars (the wasps' natural prey), two wasp faces whose features had been isolated and then randomly redistributed or, finally, two wasp faces that were missing their antennae.

The wasps learned faster to distinguish canonical faces than all other stimuli. In contrast, when face features were randomly arranged or when faces lacked antennae, discrimination was as difficult as with images of geometric shapes or caterpillars. This suggests that wasps process the features of their conspecifics' faces differently from other types of stimuli, i.e. faces would appear to be special stimuli that are treated as a separate category, not unlike faces in our own species.

Like *P. fuscatus* wasps, humans are also able to recognise faces earlier and better than other types of equally complex stimuli. And it only takes slight variations in stimuli for this ability to be lost. For example, we have difficulty recognising faces when they are upside down or when the contrast ratio is reversed, as in photographic negatives.[7]

Difficulties in facial recognition (prosopagnosia or face blindness) as a re-sult of brain lesions in certain specific areas, which include the region of the fusiform gyrus, are well known, and were masterfully and sympathetically explored by Oliver Sacks (1933–2015).[8] Less well known is that difficul-ties in face recognition are present in approximately 2 per cent of humans from birth. Some studies have shown that between 25 and 39 per cent of the variability that can be observed when comparing twins who share 100 per cent of their genes (homozygotes) or the usual 50 per cent (heterozygotes) is linked precisely to hereditary factors.[9] Genetically based variability does not only manifest itself in the deficient version – i.e. in those who suffer from face blindness – for there are also so-called "super-recognisers", individuals who in the absence of specific training appear to be extraordinarily gifted in recognising faces. This suggests that at least some congenital forms of pros-opagnosia may not represent a disease, but simply one of two extremes along the continuum of a specialised ability to recognise faces (the other extreme being that of the super-recognisers).

That the *P. fuscatus*' ability is a specialised one (i.e. an "adaptive specialisa-tion" as it is called in biology) is suggested by an important fact. The nests of *P. fuscatus* are made up of groups of queens that cooperate for survival, but also compete for reproductive dominance: the alpha queen claims the right to lay eggs, and below her there is a linear hierarchy of other queens that is determined by the outcomes of agonistic and aggressive interaction. The queens recognise each other and remember each individual's position in the dominance hierarchy, thus avoiding continually engaging in new duels with each encounter. Not so in other wasp species, which are also close relatives of *P. fuscatus*. For example, in the species *P. metricus*, nests are founded by a solitary queen, and since only the queen breeds, nest members would gain no advantage from recognising each other individually. Indeed, the facial mark-ings of *P. metricus* are very poorly differentiated, and when wasps are sub-jected to discrimination tests, they learn to recognise the faces of their mates as quickly as they recognise other types of images, such as flowers or abstract configurations. The removal of the antennae also has no effect on their ability to discriminate mates' faces. It is evident, therefore, that the discriminative abilities of *P. metricus* are not based on a specialised mechanism, but instead reflect the way these wasps process all kinds of visual stimuli (flower configu-rations, abstract geometric shapes, the appearance of caterpillars etc.).

All wasps, however, even the face-recognising *P. fuscatus*, possess mini-brains, no more and no less than those of bees: a mere million neurons. Nothing like the numbers of monkeys, crows or humans. This begs the question of whether the basic components of so-called social intelligence really require as much brain capacity as is commonly believed. If social skills were indeed the driving force behind the encephalisation of our species, how is it possible to find them in brains as tiny as those of paper wasps?

## Notes

1 M. Buiatti, E. Di Giorgio, M. Piazza, C. Polloni, G. Menna, F. Taddei, E. Baldo and G. Vallortigara (2018), "A cortical route for face-like pattern processing in human newborns". *Proceedings of the National Academy of Sciences USA*, 116: 4625–4630.

2 V. M. Reid, K. Dunn, R. J. Young, J. Amu, T. Donovan and N. Reissland (2017), "The human fetus preferentially engages with face-like visual stimuli". *Current Biology*, 27: 1825–1828.

3 A review of these studies can be found in E. Di Giorgio, J. L. Loveland, U. Mayer, O. Rosa-Salva, E. Versace and G. Vallortigara (2017), "Filial responses as predisposed and learned preferences: Early attachment in chicks and babies". *Behavioural Brain Research*, 325: 90–104; Rosa-Salva, O., Mayer, U., Versace, E., Hebert, M., Lemaire and B. S., Vallortigara, G. (2021), "Sensitive periods for social development: Interactions between predisposed and learned mechanisms". *Cognition*, 213: 104552. doi:10.1016/j.cognition.2020.104552; E. Lorenzi and G. Vallortigara (2021), "Evolutionary and neural bases of the sense of animacy". In: *The Cambridge Handbook of Animal Cognition* (eds. Allison Kaufman, Josep Call, James Kaufman), pp. 295–321, Cambridge University Press, New York.

4 J. Taubert, S. G. Wardle, M. Flessert, D. A. Leopold and L. G. Ungerleider (2017), "Face pareidolia in the rhesus monkey". *Current Biology*, 27: 2505–2509.

5 E. A. Tibbetts, S. Pandit and D. Nondorf (2018), "Developmental plasticity and the origin of novel communication systems: Individual recognition in Polistes wasps". *Evolution*, 72: 2728–2735. doi:10.1111/evo.13613

6 M. J. Sheehan and E. A. Tibbetts (2011), "Specialised face learning is associated with individual recognition in paper wasps". *Science*, 334: 1272–1275.

7 See for example P. Thompson (1980), "Margaret Thatcher: A new illusion". *Perception*, 9: 483–484; and N. George, R. J. Dolan, G. R. Fink, G. C. Baylis, C. Russell and J. Driver. (1999), "Contrast polarity and face recognition in the human fusiform gyrus". *Nature Neuroscience*, 2: 574–580.

8 O. Sacks (1985). *The Man Who Mistook His Wife for a Hat*. Summit Books, London.

9 J. B. Wilmer, L. Germine, C. F. Chabris, G. Chatterjee, M. Williams, E. Loken, K. Nakayama and B. Duchaine (2010), "Human face recognition ability is specific and highly heritable". *Proceedings of the National Academy of Sciences USA*, 107: 5238–5241.

# 4

# A BRAIN FOR ALL SEASONS

All brains are surprisingly similar. Once you have seen histological preparations of the human brain under the microscope, you will have no difficulty in recognising the nervous tissue of other animals even of species
distantly related to us, like squid and insects.

Valentino Braitenberg

In general, an increase in size is observed in areas of the brain dedicated to
very specialised functions. This is the case, for example, in animals such as
bats or dolphins, whose echolocation abilities are reflected in the increased
size of the auditory areas of their brains.

The principle that the more specialised a function is, the more brain tissue is dedicated to it, applies not only to sensory perception but extends to
learning and memory. Animals that stockpile food, hiding it in numerous
sites to retrieve it months later, have an increased brain volume in an area of
the brain known as the hippocampus, which is crucial for spatial memory.[1]
Specialised brain areas can also increase in volume with seasonal cyclicity, as
is the case, for example, in certain bird species for song structures in which
memories of many different melodies must be stored.[2]

That there must be a relationship between social behaviour and the development of certain areas of the brain, especially the cortex, is a fundamental
assumption of the theory of the social function of the intellect. The assumption, however, concerns two different aspects: one qualitative, the development of specialised capacities associated with social life, such as recognising
faces; the other quantitative, the generalised increase in capacities in relation
to the greater complexity of social life, due, for example, to a greater number
of individuals. Let us consider this second aspect first.

DOI: 10.4324/9781003491033-5

The evolutionary anthropologist Robin Dunbar has tried to ascertain whether a relationship exists in primates between the size of social groups and the volume of brains; in particular, whether more complex social life corresponds to larger brains. He proposed the hypothesis that there is a cognitive limit, which would depend on brain size, to the maximum number of individuals with whom it would be possible to maintain stable social relationships, the so-called "Dunbar's number".[3]

The researcher examined the typical size of social groups in various species of non-human primates and correlated it with the size of their cerebral cortexes. On the basis of the data thus obtained, he deduced the value of Dunbar's number for the human species, which would be approximately 150 individuals. Dunbar's number does not, however, indicate the number of people we know and remember (which may depend on the capacity of our long-term memory), but rather the number of those with whom we might have stable and lasting relationships.

At first glance, the significance of this numerical value – 150 – does not seem perspicuous. It becomes so, however, if we consider the anthropological data on the various forms of social cohesion that can be traced in today's residual human hunter–gatherer groups (Dunbar's assumption is that the size of the human cortex reached its current value around 250,000 years ago, during the Pleistocene). We find on the one hand the size of the small group, sometimes called a "band", between 30 and 50 individuals, and on the other hand that of the "tribe", between 500 and 2,500 individuals.[4] Bands are characterised by their sleeping in the open air using night camps; tribes by linguistic and geographical boundaries. Between these extremes lies the "clan", typically consisting of between 100 and 200 individuals. In some respects, the clan has elusive manifestations: the individuals belonging to it often interact for purely ritualistic purposes, with intervals that may also be very sporadic, perhaps only once a year. What characterises this intermediate-sized group, however, is that individuals meet – albeit not on a daily basis like in bands – with sufficient regularity to ensure direct personal acquaintance, and thus a bond between all members.

Dunbar believes he has identified the vestiges of this fundamental grouping in our social life today. For example, in all human armies, the smallest independent unit consists of 179.6 individuals on average; Christmas cards are sent to 153.5 individuals on average; in business organisation, groups of fewer than 150 people work best with a direct personal mode of interaction, whereas when the number increases, so does the need to establish a formal hierarchy.[5]

According to Dunbar, the relationship between brain size and cognitive functions should be seen in terms of an information processing problem: if there is more information to process, then a larger neuronal substrate is needed. Therefore, larger brains would be necessary when living in larger social groups.

Actually, increasing cognitive capacities at the level of individuals is not the only possible solution. The alternative may be to specialise groups of individuals to perform different functions. Consider the case of leafcutter ants, which collect leaves to build litter in which they cultivate fungi, and which comprise colonies of fewer than 100 monomorphic individuals or colonies containing millions of polymorphic, highly specialised individuals in castes. In these animals, as the number of individuals in the colony increases, the size of a specific structure of the nervous system, the antennal lobe, increases, but the overall relative size of the brain *decreases*.[6]

In animal societies such as primates, which are based on individuals, increased complexity in social life can be dealt with by endowing all individuals with greater brain capacity across the board (e.g. more memory space). But in societies of animals such as ants (or bees) which are caste-based, the increase in complexity in the social structure can instead be controlled by increased specialisation: each individual is given a few or even only one specialised function, while different functions are allocated to different castes. This does not require an increase in the overall neuronal endowment of individuals. Indeed, this may even be decreased as a result of specialisation: for example, the size of the antennal lobe increases, creating specialists in discrimination and olfactory memory but subtracting other functions from the rest of the brain – functions that are simply taken over by individuals of different castes.

## Notes

1 D. F. Sherry, A. L. Vaccarino, K. Buckenham and R. S. Herz (1989), "The hippocampal complex of food-storing birds". *Brain, Behavior and Evolution*, 34: 308–317.
2 F. Nottebohm (1981), "A brain for all seasons: Cyclical anatomical changes in song control nuclei of the canary brain". *Science*, 214: 1368–1370.
3 R. I. M. Dunbar (1992), "Neocortex size as a constraint on group size in primates". *Journal of Human Evolution*, 22: 469–493; R. I. M. Dunbar (1998), *Grooming, Gossip, and the Evolution of Language*. Harvard University Press, Cambridge, Mass.
4 R. I. M. Dunbar (1993), "Coevolution of neocortical size, group size and language in humans". *Behavioral and Brain Sciences*, 16: 681–735.
5 R. I. M. Dunbar (2010), *How Many Friends Does One Person Need? Dunbar's Number and Other Evolutionary Quirks*. Faber and Faber, London.
6 A. J. Riveros, M. A. Seid and W. T. Wcislo (2012), "Evolution of brain size in class-based societies of fungus-growing ants (Attine)". *Animal Behaviour*, 83: 1043–1049.

# 5

# FACES, FLOWERS AND PROFILES

To pack the Bud – oppose the Worm –
Obtain its right of Dew –
Adjust the Heat – elude the Wind –
Escape the prowling Bee

Emily Dickinson

Regardless of the quantitative aspect, i.e. whether a society is made up of many or few individuals, it could still be argued that there are *qualitatively* different, specialised and specific tasks that must be performed in connection with having a social life. We might therefore expect that, as in the case of other adaptive specialisations – from the spatial memory of birds stocking up on food to the echolocation of dolphins – some kind of neurological *surplus* accompanying the ability to recognise faces might be observed.

From the point of view of the growth of specific brain territories, however, the comparison between wasp species capable of recognising the faces of mates and species unable to do so is rather disappointing.[1] In fact, no volumetric increase is observed in the areas of the brain responsible for analysing visual stimuli. Compared with species unable to do so, those capable of recognising faces show a reduction in size in the nuclei deputed to the processing of olfactory information, which would fit with a greater role of visual information than olfactory information in social interaction, yet no difference in the nuclei given over to the processing of visual information per se.

Intuitively, recognising faces appears to us to be a demanding task, the kind of activity that may have promoted the development of large brains in the primate evolutionary line. In social insects, the complexity of the tasks performed by individuals of different castes correlates with the size of those parts

DOI: 10.4324/9781003491033-6

of the brain that we consider "associative", such as the mushroom bodies. For example, forager bees, which perform more complex tasks, at least from a sensory point of view, than their colleagues who stay in the "nurseries" and take care of the larvae, possess mushroom bodies that are about 15 per cent larger.[2] Curiously, however, *P. fuscatus*, the paper wasp species that recognises the faces of its mates, has *smaller* mushroom bodies than those of the species that do not recognise faces, perhaps because – as we have just observed – the olfactory areas are reduced and the olfactory input to the mushroom bodies is therefore also reduced. Whatever the reason, nothing special can be seen in the mushroom bodies that can be linked to the ability to recognise faces. If these wasps do possess specialised neurons for recognising faces, as has been documented in primates and other mammals, they are likely to be small or few in number, because they do not seem to contribute significantly to the size of the optic lobes or central associative areas that receive visual information like the mushroom bodies. In short, everything seems to conspire towards a surprising conclusion: no brain "extras" are required to recognise faces, and so probably all species of paper wasps are endowed with the basic equipment to analyse faces, and those species that have actually developed this ability must have done so through minimal retooling of the basic equipment.

That facial recognition may have developed without major upheavals in the neuronal architecture is also suggested by the fact that it is a capacity that has appeared at least five times, quite independently, in the evolutionary history of the genus *Polistes*.[3]

Let us now consider the case of animals that lack specialisation in facial recognition. Bees do not possess any special facial markings, from which they would, incidentally, derive no benefit at all considering that interactions with their mates take place mainly in the darkness of the hive. But are bees able to recognise faces? Would they be able to discern individual wasp faces as *P. fuscatus* does?

No one has tried to teach bees to recognise the faces of wasps, but it is very likely that they would be able to do so, because it has been shown that they are capable of distinguishing human faces, which are no less different from each other than are wasp faces.

Bees can learn to discriminate simple stimuli consisting of three elements, arranged in the form of a face or non-face, such as those used in experiments with infants (p.). They can also be trained to recognise more naturalistic stimuli, such as a photograph of one person's face as distinct from another. If features of a face are randomly mixed, bees lose the ability to recognise the face. This would prove that discrimination is not based on the mere presence of the local individual features of each face (which are always there, even if randomly shuffled), but on their precise spatial arrangement.[4] In other words, discrimination would appear to be based on the overall configuration of facial features, just as it is in human beings.

Objects have different appearances depending on the observer's point of view. A flower has a different shape seen from above or from the side. The same happens with a face seen from the front or in profile. Studies with infants suggest that they are unable to generalise, recognising images of the same face shown from the front and in profile as equal. They are able to do so, however, if the angular rotation is only 45 degrees, with the face rotated three-quarters instead of 90 degrees. After seeing a face rotated three-quarters, they are able to recognise its identity when they are shown the same face seen from the front (or vice versa, they are able to recognise a face seen from the front and then rotated three-quarters as the same).[5] This does not depend on the extent of the rotation, but on the perceptually available information in a three-quarter rotated image. In fact, after seeing a face rotated three-quarters, infants do not know how to recognise it when presented in profile (in spite of the fact that the rotation is the same as when going from a three-quarter face to a face seen from the front, i.e. 45 degrees in both cases). Adults also have difficulty generalising from faces seen from the front to those seen in profile and vice versa, plausibly due to decreased perceptual information about the internal characteristics of the face seen in profile. It seems likely that interpolation processes are at work when we recognise a face seen slightly rotated as "the same", and there is evidence that these processes are also observable in the mini-brains of bees.[6]

One group of bees was trained to discriminate frontally oriented human faces, as shown in the first column in Figure 5.1 and then tested with faces rotated 30 degrees, as in the second column of the same figure. A second group of bees underwent the same treatment but with faces oriented at 60 degrees during training and 30 degrees during the test. The angular variation between the training and test phases was therefore the same in the two groups. The third group, which represented the crucial condition, instead underwent training with both faces rotated 60 degrees and frontally oriented. The next test was conducted with faces rotated by 30 degrees. In this condition, therefore, the bees could learn to interpolate the features of faces rotated by 30 degrees on the basis of their previous experience with faces oriented frontally or rotated by 60 degrees. Only animals in this third condition showed the ability to recognise faces rotated by 30 degrees on the test.

A fourth group confirmed that the bees' performance was based on a genuine interpolation process. In this group during training, the bees learnt to recognise faces using both frontally oriented stimuli and stimuli rotated by 30 degrees. When tested, they were presented with faces rotated by 60 degrees. With regard to the variety of stimuli employed (two types of orientation) and angular variation (training from zero plus 60 and then testing with 30, or training from zero plus 30 and then testing with 60) the conditions were comparable to those of the third group in the previous experiment. However,

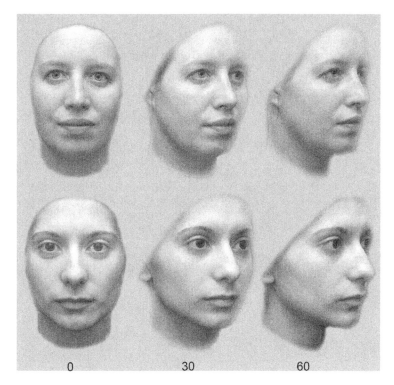

**FIGURE 5.1** Images of faces in frontal view or rotated by 30 or 60 degrees used in experiments with bees.

*Source:* Dyer, A. G. and Vuong, Q. C. (2008), "Insect brains use image interpolation mechanisms to recognise rotated objects". *PLoS ONE*, 3(12): e4086.

in this case, where they were supposed to *extrapolate* rather than *interpolate* the face shape based on their previous experience, the bees failed.

Recognising human faces is not something a bee's brain is specifically designed for. The fact that it is able to do so suggests the same mechanisms that are at work to recognise objects of biological interest to bees, such as flowers, are employed to interpolate the various views of human faces rotated at different angles, and thus recognise their invariance.

Paper wasps in nature spontaneously learn to recognise the faces of their mates and use this information in a social context. Bees, on the other hand, can learn to recognise stimuli such as human faces if they are trained to do so, i.e. in the context of associative learning, when they are rewarded for choosing the correct face. But, and this is the important point, they can do it too, with mini brains that are *not specialised* in face recognition. So, it does not seem to take large brains or particularly specialised brains to discriminate faces.

## Notes

1 W. Gronenberg, L. E. Ash and E. A. Tibbetts (2008), "Correlation between facial pattern recognition and brain composition in paper wasps". *Brain Behavior and Evolution*, 71: 1–14.
2 G. S. Withers, S. E. Fahrbach and G. E. Robinson (1993), "Selective neuroanatomical plasticity and division of labour in the honeybee". *Nature*, 364: 238–240.
3 E. A. Tibbetts (2004), "Complex social behaviour can select for variability in visual features: A case study in Polistes wasps". *Proceedings of the Royal Society B*, 271: 1955–1960.
4 A. Avarguès-Weber, G. Portelli, J. Benard, A. Dyer and M. Giurfa (2010), "Configural processing enables discrimination and categorisation of face-like stimuli in honeybees". *Journal of Experimental Biology*, 213: 593–601. See also A. Avarguès-Weber, D. d'Amaro, M. Metzler, V. Finke, D. Baracchi and A. G. Dyer (2018), "Does holistic processing require a large brain? Insights from honeybees and wasps in fine visual recognition tasks". *Frontiers in Psychology*, 9: 1313.
5 C. Turati, H. Bulf and F. Simion (2008), "Newborns' face recognition over changes in viewpoint". *Cognition*, 106: 1300–1321.
6 A. G. Dyer and Q. C. Vuong (2008), "Insect brains use image interpolation mechanisms to recognise rotated objects". *PLoS ONE*, 3(12): e4086.

# 6

# FACES OF MEMORY

Many facts seem to suggest that face discrimination in humans and other mammals is an adaptive specialisation. An example is provided by sheep. In the region of the temporal lobe, where nerve cells that respond selectively to faces are observed in both humans and monkeys, in addition to cells that respond to sheep or shepherd faces, sheep possess cells that respond specifically to the presence of horns.

It is probably also the case that for paper wasps, such as *P. fuscatus*, which treat images of mates without antennae in the same way as other stimuli, i.e. as if they were no longer special stimuli, face recognition is an adaptive specialisation. I would not be surprised if we discovered cells in their brains that selectively respond to the sight of a nice pair of antennae (akin to the "horn cells" of sheep).

Bees, on the other hand, have no specific capacity for face recognition: they recognise faces just as they recognise a flower, perhaps one with a slightly odd shape. This seems to show that an adaptive specialisation for recognising faces is not necessary: discrimination can be conducted by co-opting and reusing mechanisms that have evolved for other purposes, such as recognising flowers. Any perplexity dissolves, I believe, if we shift the emphasis from the perceptual to the memory domain. This is a point I will return to, but it is worth briefly anticipating.

What kind of function is performed by neurons that respond to faces? In other words: are these neurons there to recognise faces in general or are they rather representations of memories of specific faces? The data suggest that the second hypothesis is correct, namely that face-sensitive cells provide an explicit representation of the individual they represent. Explicit,

DOI: 10.4324/9781003491033-7

here, means that it is possible to reconstruct from the signals provided by the face neurons, which in mammals are located in the temporal lobe, to which particular individual the face belongs. At the level of the visual cortex, on the other hand, it is possible to reconstruct how the neuronal signals refer to faces and not to other types of stimuli, but without specifying which particular type of face it is.[1] If these face cells are memories of the faces of individuals, and if these memories are represented, albeit in a scattered form, by a limited number of neurons, then it becomes easy to understand why the surplus of neurons in large brains has nothing to do with information processing. The "leftover" neurons in big brains are not there for thinking – they are there instead for the mere management of large memories. To put it in computer science jargon, they are mass memory storage units, not central processing units.

Studies with so-called artificial neural networks suggest that recognising faces does not require a particularly rich endowment of neurons. A network consisting of an input grid of $32 \times 32$ elements and two levels of hidden layers each of 250 nodes ("neurons") is sufficient for a face recognition accuracy of 74.1 per cent.[2] The message is clear: a few hundred neurons are enough to recognise faces. The problem, if anything, is the memory of these faces.

Sheep, as has been proven, can learn to recognise 50 individual faces of their mates and remember them two years later.[3] Their actual capabilities are almost certainly far greater. Hens apparently remember hundreds of faces of humans as well as those of other hens.[4] In the case of humans, we can imagine that 150 (Dunbar's number) is the basic endowment for a personal, direct knowledge of other individuals, but in terms of memory capacities, it seems well established that an average person can recognise many thousands of faces.[5]

Experiments with bees or paper wasps show that, after brief training, these animals can distinguish images of two faces or the particular markings of two different conspecifics. But how many faces can they remember? I believe very few. Memory capacity could therefore be a good reason for brains with many neurons. Once again, it would not be a question of having more sophisticated processors, just larger hard disks.

There is another way, however, in which differences in memory could translate into differences in cognitive performance, because having more neurons offers the ability to perform calculations in shorter times. For example, while they can recognise elementary visual features such as the orientation of a stimulus in a few milliseconds, the recognition of complex configurations takes insects such as bumblebees longer than primates. Apes or humans can recognise complex images presented for only 20 milliseconds, whereas bumblebees need at least 100 milliseconds to do so.[6]

It could therefore be argued that mini-brains have a lower visual capacity in representational terms. In actual fact, this depends very much on the type of hypothesis one wants to support about the mechanism of vision. Theorists such as Kevin O'Regan have argued persuasively that "seeing" does not mean generating representations in the brain (which would confront us with the problem of some little man inside the brain who would have to look at these representations, and in whose brain representations a second little man would therefore have to be generated to look at them... and so on, ad infinitum); seeing would rather be something that an organism *does*, something that it *performs*.[7] As Maurice Merleau-Ponty (1908–1961) already argued, seeing is "palpation with the gaze".[8] Seeing, according to this outlook, would appear to be an exploratory activity mediated by knowledge of sensorimotor contingencies. In a sense, O'Regan argues, seeing is no different from remembering: in both cases, like in imagination, a continuous active process of questioning and control would seem to be at play, only that in vision it is the real world that serves as external memory and control.

To sample the world, animals with mini-brains need more time, because they possess fewer neurons, but in nature they can compensate for this disadvantage by very fast and very intense motor activity, as flies and midges do by moving around the environment. We only notice their limitations when we place them in unnatural conditions, preventing them from moving and thus actively exploring visual scenes, or when, in the laboratory, we present stimuli for intervals that are too short compared with those necessary for the integration of information that may be obtained sequentially over time.

## Notes

1 R. Q. Quiroga (2016), "Neuronal codes for visual perception and memory". *Neuropsychologia*, 83: 227–241. See also by the same author *Borges and Memory*, MIT Press, Cambridge, Mass., 2012. For a different story held for mechanisms to direct attention towards face-like stimuli as shown in human newborns, for which we recently found strong evidence that they are innate, see D. Kobylkov, O. Rosa-Salva, M. Zanon and G. Vallortigara (2024), "Innate face detectors in the nidopallium of young domestic chicks", bioRxiv. doi: 10.1101/2024.02.15.580445.

2 M. J. Aitkenhead and A. J. S. McDonald (2003), "A neural network face recognition system", *Engineering Applications of Artificial Intelligence*, 16: 167–176. The origin of studies on neural networks can be found in psychologist Frank Rosenblatt's "Perceptron" (F. Rosenblatt, "The perceptron: A theory of statistical separability", in *Cognitive Systems*. Cornell Aeronautical Laboratory, Report No. VG-1196-G-l, January 1958; see also H. D. Block (1962), "The Perceptron: A model for brain functioning", *Reviews of Modern Physics*, 34: 123–135. The Perceptron is a self-organising system developed on the basis of the behaviour of single, specific neural networks which, albeit in a very simplified form, are assumed to emulate the real functioning of neurons.

3 K. M. Kendrick, A. P. da Costa, A. E. Leigh, M. R. Hinton and J. W. Peirce (2001), "Sheep don't forget a face", *Nature*, 414: 165–166.

4 A. Potts (2012), *Chicken*. Reaktion Books, London.

5 R. Jenkins, A. J. Dowsett and A. M. Burton (2018), "How many faces do people know?" *Proceedings of the Royal Society of London B*, 285: 20181319, doi: 10. 1098/rspb.2018.1319.
6 V. Nityananda, P. Skorupski and L. Chittka (2014), "Can bees see at a glance?" *The Journal of Experimental Biology*, 217: 1933–1939.
7 K. J. O'Regan (2011), *Why Red Doesn't Sound Like a Bell: Explaining the Feel of Consciousness*. Oxford University Press, Oxford.
8 M. Merleau-Ponty (1945), *Phénoménologie de la perception*. Paris, Gallimard.

# 7
# BIG CONCEPTS FOR SMALL BRAINS

The fact that paper wasps *P. fuscatus* treat the faces of mates with or without antennae differently leads one to believe that they possess a "category" for such stimuli, i.e. a way of considering objects that are different as identical by grouping them together, at least for certain purposes.

Some categories, for example faces, seem to be already predisposed at birth. However, our mental life includes various perceptual categories that are formed as a result of experience. Think, for example, of the kind of practice required for an art critic to recognise a painting as belonging to a particular artist. This may rightly seem a pinnacle of human mental capabilities. And it certainly is, as far as the intricate amount of cultural-historical knowledge that can be associated with an artist's style is concerned. But what about the purely perceptive aspect? Does the glance that makes the expert say "this is a Monet painting" really call for a large brain?

The five pairs of images you see in Figure 7.1 (marked as *a*) are each composed of one painting by Monet and one by Picasso. They were chosen from a catalogue in such a way that contrast and colour were similar in each pair. Some bees were trained to discriminate between the two pictures; one half of the animals was rewarded for choosing Monet, the other half for choosing Picasso. When the animal flew to the correct image it obtained a little sugar solution, which it could find in a hole under the image, while in the hole under the wrong image, the reward was absent.

Insects quickly learnt discrimination.[1] After all, these were colourful images similar to those exhibited by flowers in nature: no wonder bees could easily tell them apart. But what if the animals were subsequently shown new pairs of images (marked as *b* in Figure 7.1), never seen before, which still consisted of one painting by Monet and one by Picasso? Despite the fact that

DOI: 10.4324/9781003491033-8

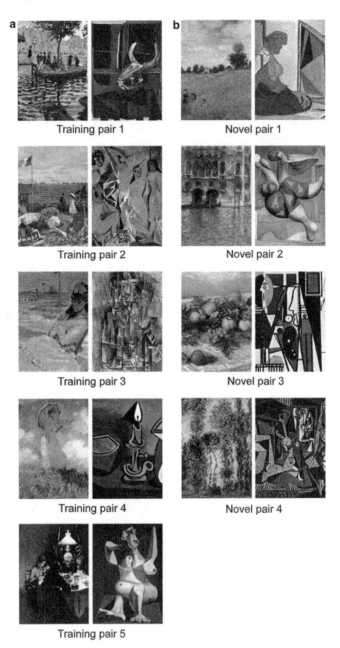

**FIGURE 7.1** Pairs of Monet and Picasso paintings used during training (a) and the subsequent test with novel stimuli (b) in bees.

*Source:* Wu, W., Moreno, A. M., Tangen, J. M. and Reinhard, J. (2013), "Honeybees can discriminate between Monet and Picasso paintings". *Journal of Comparative Physiology A*, 199: 45–55.

the images were very different, the bees still answered correctly, albeit at a lower percentage than the originals.[2]

As I noted above, no one here would argue that bees recognise a style of painting by interpreting its content semantically. The malevolent inference concluding that you only need a few neurons to be an art critic is baseless.[3] It is less baseless to conclude that the perceptual discrimination of a pictorial style is not a complex brain function that can only be observed in neuron-rich brains such as those of humans. The ability to extract and group features of complex images is accessible even to mini-brains with fewer than a million neurons. But how do they do it?

Each painting consists of such a multitude of lines, shapes, edges and colours that it is not possible to use specific elements to categorise and generalise. In theory, bees could employ more general features such as symmetry and global (or average) orientation present in the different styles. However, an analysis using vertical and horizontal filters showed that, on the whole, the two art styles contain a similar amount of information regarding orientation and symmetry. The distribution of spatial frequencies[4] also varies in the two styles in a fairly similar manner, such that it cannot be used as a reliable criterion for differentiation. The most reasonable hypothesis is that bees use the regularities that appear consistently in all paintings by the same artist. It appears that humans (but also pigeons) rely on structural regularities when discriminating faces, painting styles or photographs of natural scenes. There are computer vision techniques that, instead of relying on the characteristics of individual separate images, reduce the typical image information – lines, shapes and objects – by trying to extract the structural regularities that unite an entire set of images.[5]

Sophisticated as it may be, however, what we have discussed so far is still a *perceptual* categorisation, based on the extraction of structural characteristics that – in a statistical sense at least – are common to all specimens. However, there are abstract categories to which no common perceptual characteristics correspond. Concepts such as "equal and different", "high and low", "above and below": these entities, we have been taught, are the building blocks of thought, and human reason would find its most accomplished expression in their very existence.

Consider, however, the concept of "equal/different". In the laboratory, it is possible to document its possession using a procedure called "matching-to-sample", as shown in Figure 7.2 (left). The bee first sees a stimulus, say a yellow disc. It can then choose in a Y-shaped maze between a stimulus identical to the one just seen (yellow disc) and a new stimulus (blue disc). The experiment can be conducted in two different versions, either following the "choose the same" rule (I saw the yellow disc and so I choose the yellow one when it is presented together with the blue one) or following the "choose the different" rule (I saw the yellow disc and so I choose the blue one when it is presented together with the yellow one). As usual, the point is not to prove that bees

(a)

(b)

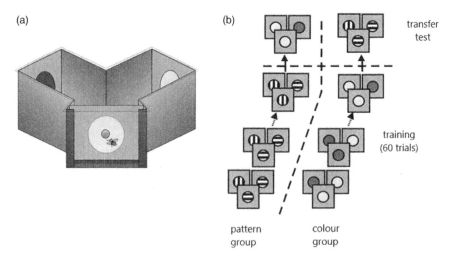

transfer
test

training
(60 trials)

pattern
group

colour
group

**FIGURE 7.2** Apparatus and procedure for studying the concept of "equal/different" in bees. In each trial, the animals must choose from the pair of stimuli presented in the T-maze the one that is the same as the stimulus shown at the entrance. The "choose the same" rule must then transfer to different aspects of the stimulus, so that, for example, bees trained to recognise the "same" colour subsequently transfer the rule to the orientation of the "same" stimulus.

*Source:* Avarguès-Weber, A. and Giurfa, M. (2013), "Conceptual learning by miniature brains". *Proceedings of the Royal Society B*, 280: 20131907.

can discriminate between the two colours – of course they can. Instead, it is a question of whether they have learnt the rule – choose the same one (or choose the different one) – because the notion of equal/different is abstract, and it applies to any pair of stimuli, even those that animals have never seen. Thus, for example, if one group of bees is trained using coloured discs and another group is instead trained using configurations of horizontal and vertical stripes as in Figure 7.2 (right), when in the generalisation test the bees trained with the differently coloured stimuli are shown the differently oriented stimuli or vice versa, the animals continue to respond according to the rule, i.e. choose the same one (or choose the different one) regardless of the fact that they have not previously had any experience with the type of stimuli used in the test.

The concept of "equal/different" is also abstract because it does not depend on a particular sensory modality. Two colours can be the same, just as two smells can be the same. In fact, bees trained to discriminate pairs of colours by following the rule "choose the same" (or different) then transfer the discrimination to pairs of odours by following the same rule.[6]

Other concepts, such as "above/below" and "right/left" were similarly explored, which, for an animal moving in a complex environment, as the bee does, are highly advantageous.[7] What is astonishing about these results is the time it takes bees to handle the concepts. About 30 trials (ca. three hours of training) are enough. Pigeons or monkeys require thousands of training trials to show the same level of abstract generalisation. Why should animals that have brains several orders of magnitude smaller than those of primates acquire categories and abstract concepts faster?

John Locke, in *An Essay Concerning Human Understanding* (1690),[8] argues that everything we experience with our senses cannot be contained in the mind, because no mind is spacious enough to accommodate the representations of each individual perception, which are manifold. In the absence of concepts, i.e. the possibility of grouping multitudes of individuals into categories, even the lexicon would explode, because we would have to represent each individual sensory experience, with a proper name.

As Borges wrote:

At a glance, we perceive: three glasses on a table. Funes: all the branches, the bunches and grapes on a pergola. He knew the shapes of the southern clouds of the dawn of 30 April 1882, and could compare them, in his memory, with the marbled cover of a book he had seen only once, or with the foam he lifted on an oar, on the Rio Negro, on the eve of the battle of Quebracho. These memories were not simple: each visual image was linked to muscular, thermal, etc. sensations. He could reconstruct the dreams of his sleep, all the images of his drowsiness. Two or three times he had reconstructed an entire day; he had never hesitated, but each reconstruction had required an entire day.[9]

Funes the Memorious, like any other human being endowed with a considerable number of neurons, can afford to take a whole day to reconstruct his memories of an entire day. Maps spanning the territory they cover have a long tradition in literature. In the short story *Sylvie and Bruno Concluded* (1893) by Lewis Carroll, the following passage can be read:

Mein Herr looked so thoroughly bewildered that I thought it best to change the subject. "What a useful thing a pocket-map is!" I remarked.

"That's another thing we've learned from your Nation," said Mein Herr, "map-making. But we've carried it much further than you. What do you consider the largest map that would be really useful?"

"About six inches to the mile."

"Only six inches!" exclaimed Mein Herr. "We very soon got to six yards to the mile. Then we tried a hundred yards to the mile. And then came the grandest idea of all! We actually made a map of the country, on the scale of a mile to the mile!"

"Have you used it much?" I enquired.

"It has never been spread out, yet," said Mein Herr: "the farmers objected: they said it would cover the whole country, and shut out the sunlight! So we now use the country itself, as its own map, and I assure you it does nearly as well.[10]

Notice how the problem does not arise from the impossibility of having an accurate record of all that is experienced. Funes, according to Borges, would indeed possess such a prodigious capacity. But even if this were true, it is hard to see how he could benefit from it. Borges says: "he had effortlessly learned English, French, Portuguese and Latin, but I suspect he was not very capable of thinking". The tragedy of Funes is that in the absence of concepts, he is unable to connect anything. If each individual experience is unique and different there is no way to put them together, to connect them. To fabricate concepts is to establish classes of equivalence, and to disregard, neglect or forget individual details. For the purpose of a certain response, whether explicitly motorised or mentally simulated (a thought), it is convenient to consider certain individuals as equivalent to each other. In this way, one is no longer disturbed, as Funes was, by the fact that "the 3.14 pm dog (seen in profile) had the same name as the 3.15 pm dog (seen from the front)" or the same name as the poodle that is now passing under my window or my mother's husky from many years ago. These are specimens of a single class, for which we can expect, with regard to all individual members, a similarity of behaviour: dog food, daily walk, leash and collar...

On the other hand, having only collections of individual entities without access to specimens would be counterproductive. There are circumstances in which I need to be able to recognise my personal dog, and so it is precisely its special characteristics that aid me with individual recognition.

Animals endowed with mini-brains face a real problem with individual memories: as they have few neurons, it is imperative for them to form concepts, building categories that group individual specimens together, neglecting details in favour of more general and invariant properties (or at least co-varying between all individuals). This leads to an expected consequence: we should not be surprised that animals endowed with mini-brains are so good at forming concepts,[11] precisely because being endowed with only a few neurons they have to be good at forming concepts. Only those with many neurons can allow themselves the luxury of memorising "the shapes of the southern clouds of the dawn of 30 April 1882", but they will not think or reason more profitably.

You don't need many neurons to think. But what would be the use of having so many neurons then? Before trying to answer, allow me a few digressions. The first, justified precisely by the value of differences in the formation of concepts.

## Notes

1 Some 30 training sessions were sufficient, each session consisting of 20 minutes of testing during which the bee usually conducted two to three trials. See W. Wu, A. M. Moreno, J. M. Tangen and J. Reinhard (2013), "Honeybees can discriminate between Monet and Picasso paintings". *Journal of Comparative Physiology A*, 199: 45–55.

2 Curiously, generalisation was better if the new images were shown in black and white rather than in colour. Apparently, the patches of colour in the new images made it difficult for the bees to enucleate the elements common to the two styles. See W. Wu, A. M. Moreno, J. M. Tangen and J. Reinhard (2013), "Honeybees can discriminate between Monet and Picasso paintings", *Journal of Comparative Physiology A*, 199: 45–55.

3 Also because the expert is usually asked to discriminate between the original and a copy; a type of task that would be interesting to study in other animals.

4 It is possible to describe any luminance distribution as a sum of sinusoidal distributions, i.e. as a sum of periodic gratings consisting of a series of bars of appropriate size (spatial frequency: number of bars per unit visual angle) and contrast. High spatial frequencies correspond to thinner bars, low spatial frequencies to wider bars.

5 An example described by the authors of the bee study is the technique of "singular value decomposition", which enables the satisfactory grouping of different images (see W. Wu, A. M. Moreno, J. M. Tangen and J. Reinhard (2013), "Honeybees can discriminate between Monet and Picasso paintings". *Journal of Comparative Physiology A*, 199: 45–55.

6 M. Giurfa, S. Zhang, A. Jenett, R. Menzel and M. V. Srinivasan (2001), "The concepts of 'sameness' and 'difference' in an insect". *Nature*, 410: 930–933; A. Avargués-Weber, A. G. Dyer, M. Combe and M. Giurfa (2012), "Simultaneous mastering of two abstract concepts by the miniature brain of bees". *Proceedings of the National Academy of Sciences USA*, 109: 7481–7486; M. Giurfa and R. Menzel (1997), "Insect visual perception: Complex abilities of simple nervous systems". *Current Opinion in Neurobiology*, 7: 505–513.

7 A. Avargués-Weber, A. G. Dyer and M. Giurfa (2011), "Conceptualisation of above and below relationships by an insect". *Proceedings of the Royal Society of London B*, 278: 898–905.

8 J. Locke (1690), *An Essay Concerning Humane Understanding* (1st ed.). Thomas Basset, London.

9 J. L. Borges ([1942]2002), "Funes the Memorious". In *The Argentina Reader* (eds. G. Nouzeilles et al.). Duke University Press, Durham, N. Carolina.

10 L. Carroll (1893), *Sylvie and Bruno Concluded*. London: Macmillan and Co. Available at: https://en.wikisource.org/wiki/Page:Carroll_-_Sylvie_and_Bruno_Concluded.djvu/207.

11 Indeed, neural network models have been developed that, on the basis of known properties of neural circuits in mushroom bodies, can learn the concept of equal/different and generalise it to different stimuli. See A. J. Cope, E. Vasilaki, D. Minors, C. Sabo, J. A. R. Marshall and A. B. Barron (2018), "Abstract concept learning in a simple neural network inspired by the insect brain". *PLoS Computational Biology*, 14(9); e1006435.

# 8

# INFORMATION LIES IN DIFFERENCES, AND OTHER FUNDAMENTAL PRINCIPLES

One aspect of the processes of categorisation is that they are based on the systematic removal of small differences, those relating to individuals, in order to draw sharp boundaries that circumscribe new superordinate entities, i.e. categories (which can then in turn become individuals in other superordinate entities). It can therefore be said that concepts and categories are *amplifiers of differences*, serving to draw sharper boundaries between the collections of individual entities that make up our experiences.

It is a general principle that information lies in differences, and that by exaggerating differences, brains benefit. We owe the understanding of this "primary principle" to the beast you see in Figure 8.1 and to the observation of a curious phenomenon by the physicist and physiologist Ernst Mach (1838–1916).[1]

The animal is the limulus (*Limulus polyphemus*), an arthropod widespread on the east coast of North America, from Maine to the Yucatan Peninsula. Although the common name recalls crab in various languages, in English the Atlantic horseshoe crab, in Japanese *kabutogani* i.e. "king crab" (the Pokémon "Kabuto" is in fact inspired by this animal), the limulus is a closer relative of spiders and scorpions than of crabs.

The phenomenon observed by Mach is reproduced in Figure 8.2. In the leftmost and rightmost parts of the figure there are two uniformly dark and light areas, while in the central part there is a uniform transition of brightness, from darker to lighter, from left to right. They appear where white turns grey a lighter coloured band, and where black turns grey a darker coloured band. These "Mach bands" have no correspondence in the physical distribution of illumination; they are created by the very way the brain works. Mach realised that the bands are due to lateral, antagonistic interaction processes between nerve elements in the retina.

DOI: 10.4324/9781003491033-9

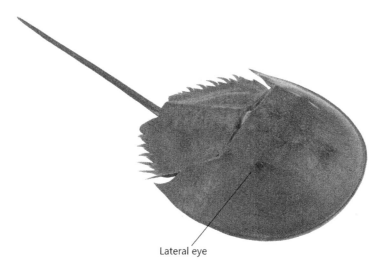

Lateral eye

**FIGURE 8.1**   The limulus (*Limulus polyphemus*). One of the two compound lateral eyes can be seen in the image.

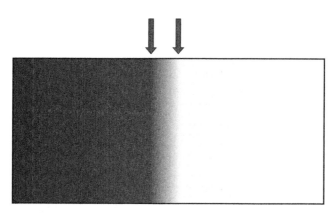

**FIGURE 8.2**   An example of the Mach band phenomenon. In the transition zone between light and dark, we see a stripe blacker than the black on the left and a stripe whiter than the white on the right.

In 1949, the physiologist Haldan Keffer Hartline first recorded the electrical activity of the nerve fibres in the ommatidia of the limulus eye.[2] As in other invertebrates, the lateral eyes of the limulus are "compound", i.e. composed of many small elements, called ommatidia, that separately receive light and generate electrical responses in their photoreceptor structures.[3] By shining a source of light onto a single ommatidium, or on several ommatidia at the same time, whether near or far from each other, one may ascertain what kind of interaction ensues at the level of the electrical response recorded in the nerve

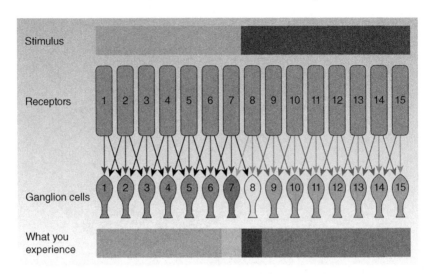

**FIGURE 8.3** The inhibitory interaction between retinal ganglion cells; see text for explanation.

fibre. Hartline discovered that the frequency of electrical impulses that can be observed in the fibre when a single ommatidium is illuminated is greatly diminished if the adjacent ommatidium is illuminated at the same time.

The genesis of the Mach bands thus becomes understandable. Receptors that are stimulated by the intermediate level of light in the transition zone receive, those closer to the lighter zone – a strong inhibition – and those closer to the darker zone, a weaker inhibition (the response of a receptor is roughly proportional to the logarithm of the stimulus intensity, and so is the inhibitory action it exerts on neighbouring receptors). The situation is shown in simplified form in Figure 8.3.

There is a sharp transition in the stimulus from left to right between a lighter and a darker grey. Receptor 7, receiving less inhibition from its right-hand neighbour (receptor 8) than its peers (1 to 6) will produce the impression of a lighter Mach band; conversely, receptor 8, receiving more inhibition from its left-hand neighbour (receptor 7) than its peers (9 to 15) will produce the impression of a darker Mach band. The net result of these lateral inhibitory interactions is that where there is an edge, a boundary in the image, i.e. a difference between two homogeneous extended surfaces, the difference will be magnified.

The ancestors of the limulus are marine arthropods that abounded in the Cambrian and of which numerous fossil remains can be found: the trilobites. Trilobites most probably possessed the mechanisms of lateral inhibition. It is therefore an ingenious device promoted by natural selection more than 500 million years ago, which we can see at work even today, not only in invertebrates with compound eyes but also in the camera eye of animals such as humans. Its function appears to be to filter out the enormous mass of data potentially available in images, discarding the redundant parts and allowing the informative ones to pass through instead.

Homogeneous surfaces do not convey information along their entire extent, it is only at the edges, where things change – in colour, brightness or texture – that information dwells with ease. This explains why simple line drawings are so effective in depicting natural scenes: visual systems have evolved to reveal edges, so as to segregate figure and ground. Line drawings, which only reveal figure–background transitions, can be traced back to the dawn of pictorial representation in human history, for instance in cave art. The lines of line drawings can also play an important function in distance and depth perception by signalling occlusion. You can see an example of this in Figure 8.4, taken from rock drawings found in South Africa, where a giraffe can be seen partially occluding another more distant one; the lines of the giraffe in the foreground thus act as a surrogate for occluding surfaces.

**FIGURE 8.4**   In the overlap zone, the contours of the giraffe on the left indicate both the margins and the depth relationship (the giraffe on the left appears to be located in front, partially occluding the one on the right).

*Source:* Kennedy, J. M. and Silver, J. (1974), "The surrogate functions of lines in visual perception: Evidence from antipodal rock and cave artwork sources". *Perception*, 3: 313–322.

Other primary principles can be traced back to organisms that possess brains with only a limited number of neurons. One of these concerns the cunning use of time delay. It is worth mentioning because it will be useful later on.

Two young German soldiers meet during the Second World War, in 1944. They are a 21-year-old biology student, Bernhard Hassenstein, and a 19-year-old aspiring physics student, Werner Reichardt. They promise each other that, if they survive the war, they will achieve something great together, founding the first research institute that brings physics and biology together.

Hassenstein was a student of Erich von Holst, a character I will tell you about shortly. Reichardt, on the other hand, with his knowledge of physics, had been recruited as a radio technician in the German air force. He came into contact with elements of the Resistance and worked to set up a radio link with the Allied army. Discovered and arrested by the Gestapo, he managed to escape and hide in Berlin until the end of the war.

It was only many years later, in 1958, that the two friends crowned the dream of their youth by starting a research group in cybernetics at the Max-Planck-Institute of Biology in Tübingen; from this original nucleus, the Max Planck Institute for Biological Cybernetics was founded in 1968. Between the end of the war and the founding of the institute, studying the optokinetic response of the *Chlorophanus* cockroach, the two friends developed a model for motion perception that still influences research into the neuroscience of vision today, and has shown its validity in all organisms, from the fly to humans.

The optomotor response manifests itself in an animal's tendency to chase a shifting configuration while on the move, so as to keep its environment perceptually stable, avoiding the impression of being subjected to a passive movement (as happens when you are standing at a station and, as you look out of the window of your carriage, the train next to yours starts to move, producing the sensation that you are moving in the opposite direction).

The cockroach was secured by Hassenstein and Reichardt with cardboard and a clothes peg, so that it was prevented from moving its body, head or eyes. However, the animal could still express its perception of the environment, even though it was constrained to remain anchored in place, by moving its legs over the surfaces of a Y-shaped globular maze (see Figure 8.5). Placed inside a rotating cylinder whose inner surface was composed of black-and-white vertical stripes, the cockroach tended to move in order to keep its visual environment stable, and its choices for the left and right surfaces at Y-shaped intersections revealed its intention to turn in a particular direction.

The mechanism that drives the optomotor response, Hassenstein and Reichardt discovered, is based on a very simple idea: "delay and compare". The light signal arriving at a photoreceptor is delayed by a filter and then multiplied by the instantaneous signal derived from the light signal of the adjacent photoreceptor.

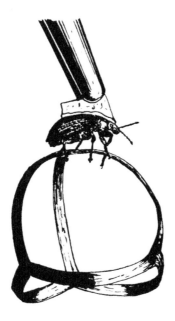

**FIGURE 8.5**   The cockroach *Chlorophanus* as it moves, bound, along Hassenstein and Reichardt's Y-maze.

*Source:* Hassenstein, B. (1991), "Der Biologe Bernhard Hassenstein", in *Freiburger Universitäts-blätter*, 114: 85–112 (Rombach, Freiburg, Germany); see also Borst, A. (2000), "Models of motion detection". *Nature Neuroscience* Supplement, vol. 3, pp. 11–68.

Suppose a strip of the rotating cylinder moves in front of the animal from right to left (Figure 8.6); by doing so, it first stimulates the receptor whose signal is delayed and then the one whose signal is not delayed. The comparator thus receives two signals which will be multiplied; the two signals will be more similar the greater the speed of the stimulus movement. Conversely, suppose the strip moves from left to right: the first signal arrives at the comparator, but there is no delayed signal with which to multiply it and the result will be null. The mechanism will therefore be able to discriminate the direction of movement, as it will only respond to stimuli moving from right to left, and through multiplication it will be sensitive to the speed of the movement (the faster the stimulus, the greater the signal leaving the comparator).[4]

Again, the mechanism identified in the simple oculomotor system of an animal such as the cockroach has been shown to operate in exactly the same manner in the mammalian brain, including, of course, that of humans.

The fact that these artifices are present in the constitution of the simplest nervous systems leads one to wonder whether in the distant past of the earliest animals must also reside the computational contrivance to which we owe the triggering of the greatest wonder: consciousness. Before I try to convince

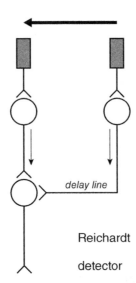

**FIGURE 8.6**  The Hassenstein and Reichardt motion detector (now universally known as the "Reichardt detector"). Two stimuli reach the receptors in grey one after the other and stimulate two neurons, the activity of one of which is delayed in relation to the other so that it reaches a comparator at the same time. The arrow indicates the direction of movement preferred by the detector.

you of this, as I realise the step is not a short one, let us return to the question about small and large brains.

If so much – in terms of information processing, and thus also of variety and flexibility in behaviour – can be achieved with hardware as modest as that available to a bee or a fly, what would be the point of having large brains with so many neurons?

## Notes

1  E. Mach (1886), *Die Analyse der Empfindungen und das Verhältnis des Physischen zum Psychischen* [The analysis of sensations and the relationship between the physical and the psychological]. Gustav Fischer, Jena.
2  H. K. Hartline (1949), "Inhibition of activity of visual receptors by illuminating nearby retinal elements in the Limulus Eye", *Federation Proceedings*, 8: 69.
3  In addition to the pair of lateral eyes, the limulus possesses simple light-sensitive eyes, two located medially, two laterally and another in an endo-parietal position.
4  The motion detector employs a short-term memory that delays the signal from one receptor relative to the other, a multiplier and a mechanism that averages the signal output from the multiplier over a certain period of time. The average of the product will have a value that increases with increasing speed. For a more complete description, see V. Braitenberg (1977), *On the Texture of Brains*. Springer Verlag, Berlin.

# 9

# NEURONS LARGE AND SMALL, IN VARIOUSLY CROWDED SPACES

How nice it would be to glide
through our hidden hives.
I would love to be that microscopic bee
sinking between the neurons
dendrites, microglia,
oligodendroglia.
Beating between the axons,
sucking drops of serotonin,
the pollen of our dreams,
and pouring it into the synapses.
Knowing how to plug holes,
drinking thoughts,
with the honey of a new soul.

Filippo Strumia

Although there have been numerous attempts over the years to correlate the size of brains with their cognitive sophistication, there are reasons to doubt that the many variations of different brain size indicators, be they absolute or relative, are of any use. This is because the brain is a complex tissue, consisting of various elements that may be present in different numbers, sizes and densities, both locally and overall. All this leads us to reconsider certain narratives about the relationship between brain size and intelligence in different species.

Take the case of cetaceans. The great intelligence attributed to these animals is often inferred from the large volume of their brains. In reality, those of different species vary in size – from the Indus dolphin's meagre one and a half ounces to the humpback whale's remarkable seven kilos. If, instead of absolute brain size, one measures the so-called encephalic quotient, which

DOI: 10.4324/9781003491033-10

takes into account the relative weight of a species' brain compared with the relative weight of the brains of species of similar size, the values turn out to be rather high in some species (4.95 for the rough-toothed dolphin), but rather modest in others (0.16 for sperm whales). How to explain such differences? Neuroanatomist Paul Manger has suggested that the explanation may have nothing to do with intelligence, but with the problem of keeping the brain at the right temperature for it to function well in a medium, water, where heat dissipation is rapid. In cetacean species that have large brains, one does not observe a great density of neurons, but rather an unusually high number of glial cells, which may indeed serve for better thermal control. Confirming this, Manger showed that the larger the brains, the colder the waters of the seas inhabited by the various cetacean species.[1]

However, the idea of the encephalic quotient also encounters difficulties regardless of the composition of brain tissue. If we limit ourselves to considering nerve cells alone, one factor influencing the size of brains is in fact the size of the cells themselves, which are in general the larger the animal. But that's not all: the density of nerve cells can be different in different species, as we have seen in the case of dolphins.

Let me relate an enlightening story in this regard. A few years ago, a young Brazilian student, Suzana Herculano-Houzel, began pestering the leading experts in comparative neuroanatomy by asking them at congresses and conferences what the original scientific work was which showed that the number of neurons in the human brain is 100 billion. Despite the fact that this value is incessantly quoted in textbooks (and journalistic pieces), Suzana Herculano-Houzel soon realised that there was no convincing data to back it up. The traditional method of estimating how many neurons there are in a brain is to take a slice of nerve tissue, colour it, count how many neurons it contains and then extrapolate that value to the whole brain. The procedure is inaccurate for several reasons. First, not all neurons are always visible in the slices; for example, slices coloured using the method invented by the anatomist Camillo Golgi, the so-called black reaction,[2] only show a few (and nobody knows exactly which ones and why). Moreover, the density of neurons is not the same in different parts of the brain: the cerebellum alone, for example, contains more than half the total number of neurons in certain species despite being barely half the size of the rest of the brain.

Suzana Herculano-Houzel developed a new, simple and ingenious method for counting neurons.[3] It consists of dissolving the membranes of the cells, leaving only the nuclei suspended in a kind of homogeneous soup ("isotropic", i.e. equal in all directions in terms of its density). Since each cell in the brain contains only one nucleus, counting nuclei is equivalent to counting cells. In the soup, the nuclei of neurons and other brain cells (the glia) can be easily distinguished by using methods that allow them to be coloured differently.[4] In this way, it was possible to establish that the neurons in the human brain number about 86 billion (in terms of order of magnitude, there is no difference between 100 billion and 86 billion; however, I don't know about you, but I rather resent losing 14 billion neurons in one fell swoop). The Herculano-Houzel method thus makes it possible to accurately compare the number of neurons in different species. In particular, it is possible to assess the density with which the neurons are packed in relation to the absolute size of the brains.

It has thus been observed that as brain size varies, the number of neurons can change differently in different species. In primates, neurons increase at the same rate as brains increase. If we take a gram of brain from a small-sized monkey and a gram from a large-sized one, we will find the same number of neurons inside. In rodents, however, the size of the brains increases more than the number of neurons increases. If we take a gram of rodent brain from a small-sized species, we might find that it contains *more* neurons than a gram of brain from a larger one.

The fact that in all primates the number of neurons increases at the same rate as brain size increases shows that, in this respect, the human brain is nothing special: it has exactly the number of neurons that we would expect to find in a primate with a brain of its size. If, argues Herculano-Houzel, the brain size of a chimpanzee were to increase to the size of our brain, it would also have, roughly speaking, 86 billion neurons.

Other animals, however, show a higher density of neurons than primates. For example, parrots and crows have about twice as many neurons as monkeys of similar weight, particularly in the pallium, the dorsal, outermost region of the brain, which corresponds to what in mammals is called the cortex.[5]

Herculano-Houzel is now counting neurons in the brains of insects and other invertebrates. We do not yet know the results, but already with traditional methods, it could be observed that the neurons of the mushroom bodies in bees are 5 to 20 times more densely packed than those in the brain of a mouse[6] (and it must also be taken into account that insect neurons are much smaller than those of mammals).

The advantages of large brains become apparent if we are willing to accept that they are not to be correlated with intelligence. Or if we are willing to annex to the circle of genuine forms of intelligence abilities that we do not usually consider as such; for example, visual acuity.

A limiting factor in visual acuity is the size of the optical system and receptors. Flies have compound eyes consisting of about 3,000 individual lenses, the ommatidia, which send the image to eight underlying receptors that detect light intensity and wavelength levels. Larger insects such as dragonflies can reach 30,000 ommatidia; smaller insects, such as fruitflies, stop at around 700. One advantage of the camera eye, like that of vertebrates, over the compound eye of insects is the greater number of receptive elements: in the human species, the fovea alone can contain 7 million (cones) and the remaining part of the eye 150 million (rods). Biologist Kuno Kirschfeld has

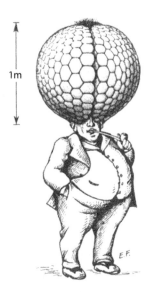

**FIGURE 9.1**  To have the same resolution as a camera eye, a person would have to possess a compound eye with a diameter of one metre.

*Source:* Kirschfeld, K. (1974), "The absolute sensitivity of lens and compound eyes". *Zeitschrift fur Naturforschung*, 29: 592–596.

calculated that in order to have a compound fly eye with the same acuity as a human's camera eye, it would have to be enlarged to a diameter of about one metre (Figure 9.1).[7]

However, the image in Figure 9.1 runs the risk of being misleading if one tries to transfer it to its dipteran reverse: a fly carrying a pair of vertebrate camera eyes would not in fact be satisfied with a simple increase in the size of its head (and thus of its body, to be able to hold such a head). It would also have to be endowed with all the indispensable neuronal circuitry inside its head. An increased number of receptors alone is meaningless if one does not also have an adequate number of neurons in the retina and the subsequent stations of the visual system to process the signal (not only in the direction from the periphery to the centre, but also in the opposite direction because, for example, about 10 per cent of the optic nerve fibres convey signals back from the cortex to the retina; which means that more fibres depart from the cortex towards the retina than towards the hand).[8]

In short, to perform a seemingly simple function like resolving images more accurately, that is, to have better visual acuity, you need a lot more neurons. The same applies to other aspects of vision, such as processing speed or the amplitude of frequencies to which one is able to respond, or any other sensory process. And it is obviously also true for the motor counterpart, because just as larger sensory organs require an increase in the number of neurons, larger muscles require more motor neurons and axons with larger diameters to travel greater distances.

This does not exactly sound like what we are used to labelling as "intelligence". It is more a question of performing functions better from a quantitative point of view that are always the same from a qualitative point of view.

Obviously, a greater number of neurons increases the redundancy of the system, and thus also offers the possibility of greater functional diversification. In fact, however, functional diversification is mainly an advantage for those with *few* neurons. A good example is provided by asymmetry in nervous systems.

When I was observing my antlions, I still did not know their brains could show left–right asymmetry. I learned of this recently, but with relatively little surprise because the data in favour of the existence of laterality phenomena in insects have been piling up over the years.[9] In antlions, a relationship between a very curious type of asymmetry and the ability to learn has been documented.[10] The direction in which antlions larvae roll over to get back on their feet after being placed belly up has been measured. The animals show a stable and reliable preference: some roll to the right, others to the left. The strength of this asymmetry, however, varies from individual to individual. You will remember (p. 11) how the larvae of the antlions learn to associate the presence of a vibratory stimulus with the arrival of prey. Well, surprisingly, the more asymmetrical an animal is in rolling over to right itself, the better it is at learning the association between the vibratory stimulus and the subsequent arrival of prey.

There are numerous other examples of the advantages that the possession of a slight right–left asymmetry seems to confer on animals. Chimpanzees fishing for termites with a severed twig are much more efficient at catching their prey when they are right- or left-handed than when they use both limbs indifferently. Pigeons are all the better at learning to discriminate visual stimuli the more they tend to use one particular eye, usually the left, to accomplish the task.[11] Domestic fowl chicks that have to cope with two tasks simultaneously, such as finding food grain scattered among pebbles on the ground while paying attention to flying predators, are better at finding food and spotting the predator when they have asymmetrical brains. They can in fact use one eye and the hemisphere on the opposite side of the head to perform one task, and the other eye and hemisphere to perform the second task.

In his novel *Origin*, Dan Brown hypothesises that the protagonist, futurologist and computer expert Edmond Kirsch succeeds in making substantial progress in the programming of his artificial intelligence when he equips it with a "bicameral" intelligence.[12] Only some 20 years ago, it was thought that the possession of a bicameral mind – with the left and right parts of the encephalon performing different functions – was a distinguishing characteristic of the human species.[13] Instead, it is such a general organisational principle that it can be observed in very tiny brains, such as that of the nematode worm *Caenorhabditis elegans*, which possesses 302 neurons in total.[14]

A fine example is provided by a class of taste cells, called ASE, which consist of a pair of neurons located on the head of the worm, one on each side, morphologically symmetrical but functionally asymmetrical in the way they respond to certain substances. The left neuron (ASEL) attracts the worm to sodium, while the right neuron (ASER) attracts chlorine and potassium.[15] By specialising the neurons so that the right and left neurons do different things – in this case respond to different types of salts – it is possible to increase the diversification of functions even in a nervous system characterised by a very small number of neurons.

Neurobiologists Lars Chittka and Jeremy Niven have pointed out a difficulty in attempts to relate the size of the brains of different species to their cognitive abilities.[16] Relative volume, usually expressed in a form that takes into account how much the brain grows in relation to the body, the so-called encephalic quotient (p. 49), is used almost universally. But as Chittka and Niven observe, for the purposes of information storage processes, it is the absolute numbers that count, not the relative ones: to be precise, the absolute number of neurons and the way they are connected.

It may be useful to return to the example of birds. We know that birds such as pigeons show performance comparable to that of monkeys or humans in quite sophisticated tasks, such as orthographic processing.[17] For example, pigeons have to decide whether or not the four-letter sequence "URSP" is a well-formed word. The term "orthographic processing", when referring to pigeons, risks being misunderstood. It is obviously not a question of pigeons understanding the spelling of a language such as Italian or English, although what they manage to do is nevertheless remarkable.

The animals have been trained to recognise as correct a certain number of words, consisting of four-letter strings actually present in the English language, in this case 58, out of a total number of 8,000 non-words of equal length. Each time a well-formed word appears on the screen, the bird can peck the symbol and thus receive a little birdseed as a reward. The pigeon could simply memorise the 58 words slavishly. Or, and this would be more interesting, it could learn that in the succession of letters presented, certain combinations are more likely than others. In a bigram of the English language, the sequence CZ would hardly ever appear, while the sequence CA would be frequent. After the training has been completed, to find out what the pigeon has learnt, it is sufficient to present it with new words. The results reveal that pigeons do indeed discriminate between new words and non-words. In addition to showing a sensitivity to the occurrence frequencies of bigrams, animals also exhibit other traits characteristic of orthographic processing, such as the transposition effect. Humans often interpret as words non-words into which adjacent letters have been transposed, e.g., in English, "*very*" transposed into "*vrey*". The same, it has been seen, happens in pigeons.

All this is interesting, but it puts us in a difficult situation from a comparative point of view. For it is true, as we have noted, that birds have a much higher density of neurons than we might expect from their small brains. If we take one gram of brain in a monkey and one gram in a parrot, the bird may have *relatively* many more neurons than the monkey. Nevertheless, even taking size and density into account, overall the absolute number of neurons in a pigeon's brain is modest compared with that of a monkey. So how does the pigeon manage to do what the monkey does? Theoretically, in terms of absolute number of neurons, small brains can still function well if they have circuit advantages over large brains with a greater overall number of neurons. For example, if nerve cells are less dense in the human cerebral cortex than in its avian analogue, the average distance between two neurons in a bird brain will be less than that in a human brain. Therefore, when populations of cells representing different aspects of a cognitive task need to communicate rapidly with each other, they may do so more quickly in a bird's brain.

## Notes

1 P. R. Manger (2013), "Questioning the interpretations of behavioral observations of cetaceans: Is there really support for a special intellectual status for this mammalian order?". *Neuroscience*, 250: 664–696. On the alleged high intelligence of dolphins on the behavioural side, see also J. Gregg (2013), *Are Dolphins Really Smart?* Oxford University Press, Oxford, UK. See also L. Vozza and G. Vallortigara (2015), *Piccoli equivoci tra noi animali* [Small misunderstandings between us animals]. Zanichelli, Bologna.

2 Because it causes a black colouring of the neurons. The technique, based on an impregnation of nerve tissue with chromium, was perfected by Santiago Ramon y Cajal. Basically, portions of the nervous system are immersed in a 2.5 per cent solution of potassium dichromate for a period of 1 to 50 days, and then immersed in a 0.5–1 per cent solution of silver nitrate. The preparations are then dehydrated, usually with ethyl alcohol, and cut into slices about 100 microns thick.

3 S. Herculano-Houzel (2016), *The Human Advantage: A New Understanding of How Our Brain Became Remarkable*. MIT Press, p. 302, Cambridge, Mass.

4 Two dyes are added to the samples: one fluorescent blue (DAPI), which binds strongly to the DNA of all the cells in the soup; and one fluorescent red (NeuN), which binds only to the nerve cells. By subtracting the estimates obtained with the two dyes, it is then possible to know the number of neurons in proportion to the total number of cells present in the brain (glial, endothelial or ependymal).

5 S. Olkowicz, M. Kocourek, R. K. Lucan, M. Portes, T. W. Fitch, S. Herculano-Houzel and P. Nemec (2016), "Birds have primate-like numbers of neurons in the telencephalon", *Proceedings of the National Academy of Sciences USA*, 113: 7255–7260.

6 W. Witthöft (1967), "Absolute Anzahl und Verteilung der Zellen im Hirn der Honigbiene" [Absolute number and distribution of cells in the honeybee brain]. *Zeitschrift Morphologie der Tiere*, 61: 160–184; D. B. Tower (1954), "Structural and functional organization of mammalian cerebral cortex: The correlation of neurone density with brain size". *Journal of Comparative Neurology*, 101: 19–51; S. E. Fahrbach, T. Giray and G. E. Robinson (1995), "Volume changes in the mushroom bodies of adult honeybee queens". *Neurobiology of Learning and Memory*, 63: 181–191.

7 K. Kirschfeld (1974), "The absolute sensitivity of lens and compound eyes". *Zeitschrift fur Naturforschung*, 29: 592–596.

8 N. Humphrey (1992), *A History of the Mind*. Chatto and Windus, London.

9 For a general review of how extensive the asymmetry between the two halves of the nervous system is in the animal kingdom, see L. J. Rogers, G. Vallortigara and R. J. Andrew (2013), *Divided Brains*. Cambridge University Press, New York; "Left-right asymmetries of behaviour and nervous system in invertebrates". *Neuroscience and Biobehavioral Reviews*, 36: 1273–1291; L. J. Rogers and G. Vallortigara (2015), "When and why did brains break symmetry?". *Symmetry*, 7: 2181–2194; G. Vallortigara and L. J. Rogers (2020), "A function for the bicameral mind". *Cortex*, 124: 274–285, doi:10.1016/j.cortex.2019.11.018.

10 K. Miler, K. Kuszewska and M. Woyciechowski (2017), "Larval antlions with more pronounced behavioural asymmetry show enhanced cognitive skills". *Biology Letters*, Published 1 February 2017, doi:10.1098/rsbl.2016.0786.

11 You will note that the advantage is individual-specific and therefore it should make no difference to favour the right or left side. In fact, however, in many species asymmetries are "directional", i.e. the majority of (but not all) individuals favour a particular direction (the classic example is of course the preference for the right hand in the majority of the human population. I have discussed elsewhere my hypothesis as to why directional asymmetry evolved. See G. Vallortigara (2006), "The evolutionary psychology of left and right: Costs and benefits of lateralisation". *Developmental Psychobiology*, 48: 418–427; G. Vallortigara and L. J. Rogers (2005), "Survival with an asymmetrical brain: Advantages and disadvantages of cerebral lateralization". *Behavioral and Brain Sciences*, 28: 575–589; S. Ghirlanda and G. Vallortigara (2004), "The evolution of brain lateralization: A game theoretical analysis of population structure". *Proceedings of the Royal Society B*, 271: 853–857; G. Vallortigara and E. Versace (2017), "Laterality at the neural, cognitive, and behavioral levels". *APA Handbook of Comparative Psychology: Vol. 1. Basic Concepts, Methods, Neural Substrate, and Behavior*, J. Call (ed.), pp. 557–577. American Psychological Association, Washington DC; E. Frasnelli and G. Vallortigara (2018), "Individual-level and population-level lateralization: Two sides of the same coin". *Symmetry*, 10, 739.

12 The reference is to the imaginative book by experimental psychologist Julian Jaynes (1976), *The Origins of Consciousness in the Breakdown of the Bicameral Mind*. Boston, Mass., Houghton Mifflin, in which the hypothesis is developed according to which the right hemisphere was, until around 1000 BC, inhabited by the "voices of the gods". See also J. Jaynes (1995), "The diachronicity of consciousness". In G. Trautteur (ed.), *Consciousness: Distinction and Reflection*. Bibliopolis, Naples.

13 Some human cognitive neuropsychologists still support this, apparently unaware of the facts of biology (see e.g. http://wuwm.com/post/roots-consciousness-were-two-minds#stream/0).

14 To be precise, in *C. elegans* there are two sexes, the hermaphrodites having exactly 302 neurons and the males having 385 (see M. Sammut, S. Cook, K. Nyguyen, T. Felton, D. Hall, S. Emmons, R. J. Poole and A. Barrios (2015), "Glia-derived neurons are required for sex-specific learning in *C. elegans*". *Nature*, 526: 385–390).

15 B. Vidal and O. Hobert (2017), "Methods to study nervous system laterality in the *Caenorhabditis elegans* model system". *Lateralised Brain Functions. Methods in Human and Non-Human Species* (L. J. Rogers and G. Vallortigara, eds.). Springer Nature, Humana Press, New York, pp. 591–608.

16 L. Chittka and J. Niven (2009), "Are bigger brains better?". *Current Biology*, 19: R995–R1008.

17 D. Scarf, K. Boy, A. Uber, R. J. Devine, O. Güntürkün and M. Colombo (2016), "Orthographic processing in pigeons". *Proceedings of the National Academy of Sciences USA*, 113: 11272–11276.

# 10

# THE BOUNDARIES OF INTELLIGENCE

perhaps a keystone principle emerging
from our research lies in the opposing laws
of nature, on the edge of chance
just as to be is to not to be,
as they are mirrored in the world of mathematical reality
like the sky at sunset in the sea;
and which owes to other form of existence
and its mysterious pure glow,
of those two worlds, it is useless to ask

Sergio Doraldi (pseudonym of Sergio Doplicher)

The absolute number of neurons, as we have noted, may be less important than how those neurons are connected. A greater absolute number of neurons may, however, amplify the brain's memory endowment. However, one must also consider the other side of the coin: any increase in the number (and size) of neurons increases consumption and reduces the energy efficiency of information processing.

The grandfather of the neurosciences, the Spaniard Santiago Ramón y Cajal (1852–1934), used to compare the circuit of neurons dedicated to vision in insects to a pocket watch. Compared with the sophisticated miniaturisation of the insect brain, the mammalian brain seemed to him to be a parlour clock, bulky and noisy. But, in fact, the construction of brains – as with any other biological structure – reflects a trade-off between relative advantages and disadvantages.

As the size of a brain increases, neurons become larger on average, which allows the number of connections per neuron to increase as the total number

DOI: 10.4324/9781003491033-11

of neurons grows. However, larger cells are crammed in less densely; and to cope with this problem, the length of the axons connecting the cells must be increased. But longer axons also take longer to transmit signals, and so, to keep the speed within acceptable limits, it is necessary to increase the thickness of the axons so as to reduce the signal transmission time.

Miniaturisation could be a solution: possessing smaller and smaller, densely packed neurons that, being close to each other, can talk to each other quickly. Even better if these small neurons were connected by thin axons that could still transmit quickly and over long distances. But even the road to miniaturisation encounters obstacles, probably insurmountable at some point, because there are *physical* limits to intelligence, as neurobiologist Simon Laughlin has shown.[1]

The limitations are associated with noise, and thus the inaccuracy of ion channels. Channels are used by neurons to generate electrical impulses and can be conceptualised – simplifying somewhat – as valves, which open and close by exploiting changes in the molecular conformation of the proteins they are made of. When the channels open, ions (e.g., sodium, calcium, potassium) can cross the cell membrane and thus generate the differences in potential between external and internal on which the electrical part of the communication between neurons is based. The problem is that being so small, ion channels sometimes open by accident. In Laughlin's words, "If you make the spring on the channel too loose, then the noise keeps on switching it. If you make the spring on the channel stronger, then you get less noise," he says, "but now it's more work to switch it."[2] In other words, there is a relationship between energy consumption and noise, and if you reduce the size of the neurons too much, you also reduce the number of channels available for signal transmission, and this increases noise.

In a provocative article published in 1980 in the journal *Science*, the question was raised as to whether the brain was really necessary.[3] The neurologist John Lorber drew attention to a number of cases of individuals with hydrocephalus: for example, that of a young mathematics student with an IQ of 126, and a completely normal social and emotional life, who, instead of the usual 4–5 centimetres of thickness between the ventricles and the surface of the cortex, showed a millimetre or so on brain scans. This may have been a completely exceptional case, but the cognitive scientist John Skoyles compiled an impressive case history of microcephalic individuals, due to hydrocephaly or hemispherectomy, who show near-normal intelligence despite possessing brains whose size is not unlike that of *Homo erectus* (around 900 $cm^3$ instead of the usual 1,300 $cm^3$).[4]

The brain, as is well known, is a metabolically very expensive tissue: it makes up just 2 per cent of the body's weight but consumes 20 per cent of the entire body's energy resources. Why then have larger brains evolved if individuals can have normal intelligence without being endowed with large brains? The answer, according to Skoyles, should be sought in the development of specialised skills.

The father of the IQ test, the French experimental psychologist Binet, whom we previously met in his youth when he was removing the sub- and supra-oesophageal ganglia of cockroaches (p. 13), excluded a fundamental talent from the outset: the ability to learn a particular skill in depth over a long period of time, so as to have total mastery over it. In modern society, an example of such an expert skill may be represented by a chess grandmaster. Clearly, this is a kind of skill that, also for reasons of time, must have been of little relevance for survival in the history of our species. However, this is not the case for many other expert skills. Studies of today's remnant hunter-gatherer societies have revealed how crucial the development of highly specialised skills, often formed over decades, is for activities such as hunting, gathering, artefact construction and even social communication. On the basis of a single paw print, an experienced hunter-gatherer can determine what animal passed by, how long ago, its sex and age, and whether it was in good physical condition or sick.

The idea that extra brain endowment – i.e. one beyond the values associated with an asymptote in measures of intelligence – might be useful for the development of specialised skills is very interesting. It parallels what we have observed about the problem posed by an increase in the number of individuals in the social group. It is possible to compensate for the increased memory load by means of caste specialisation, that is, with individuals endowed with specialised skills, as is the case in hymenoptera, or by a greater endowment of a generalist type, conferred, however, on all individuals, as is the case in vertebrates (p. 25). One way to test Skoyles' hypothesis would be to investigate whether these individuals with reduced brain endowments but normal IQs have limited capacities to develop expert skills, or whether they can only learn a limited number of them compared with individuals with normal brain endowments.

This is not the only hypothesis, of course. There is alternatively that of the grandparents.[5] The brain is a fragile organ; by middle age it has certainly already suffered structural damage. The fact that, in most people, this damage does not manifest itself in a deterioration of cognitive functions reveals how redundant the brain is. The redundancy, according to the hypothesis, is linked to life expectancy, i.e. the brain would have much more material at its disposal than is strictly necessary to enable it to maintain good cognitive function in old age, when one is at the grandparenting stage.

Broadening the horizon to comparisons between different species, the idea that the large brains of some animals may simply be very redundant, for reasons related to the capacity of memory stores and the lifespan of the animals themselves (the two are obviously related) seems very plausible.

If this is the case, there is no reason to believe the foundations of mental life are connected to a critical threshold of a size or complexity of the nervous system. On the contrary, it should be possible to enucleate these fundamentals more easily where nerve structures occur in an essential state, as must have been the case with the earliest animals, in order to try to understand the reasons for the appearance of sentient creatures.

## Notes

1 For a review of these studies, see J. E. Niven and S. B. Laughlin (2008), "Energy limitation as a selective pressure on the evolution of sensory systems". *Journal of Experimental Biology*, 211: 1792–1804.
2 See D. Fox (2011), "The limits of intelligence". *Scientific American*, July 2011, pp. 37–43.
3 R. Lewin (1980), "Is your brain really necessary?". Science, 210: 1232–1234.
4 J. R. Skoyles (1999), "Human evolution expanded brains to increase expertise capacity, not IQ". *Psycoloquy*, 10(002). To the cases associated with the pathologies should be added the variability observed in normal individuals subjected to brain scans; Skoyles reports in this regard that the variation can go well below 1000 cc (and at the other extreme reach 2000 cc).
5 N. Humphrey (1999), "Why human grandmothers may need large brains: Commentary on Skoyles on brain-expertise". *Psycoloquy*, 10: 024.

# 11

# A MINIMALIST APPROACH TO THE ISSUE OF CONSCIOUSNESS

Offer proof, if it could be found,
that God was not.

G. Boccaccio

On 17 June 2015, an open letter[1] signed by five eminent brain scholars – among them Antonio Damasio and Oliver Sacks – addressed to Christof Koch – a neuroscientist expert in consciousness studies and columnist for the journal – was published in *Scientific American*. The letter refers to an as yet unanswered question: "What characteristics of living cells lead ultimately to the various, higher-level psychological phenomena that are apparently unique to certain animal organisms?"

The authors' solution foregrounds a specific property of the cell: "we suggest that the lowest-level candidate mechanism for this analysis is that of membrane 'excitability': the unusual ability of certain types of living cells to detect and respond to stimuli within milliseconds".

Crucial to the constitution of the cell is the existence of a membrane, a boundary, that marks the difference between what is inside and what is outside. And fundamental, therefore, are the mechanisms that allow various ions to penetrate through microscopic openings: the barrier that surrounds the cell and its contents.

All cells have membranes, which preside over the exchange of materials and energy with the outside world. Thus, the authors continue, metabolic activity, biochemical homeostasis or the mere presence of a boundary

DOI: 10.4324/9781003491033-12

between the cellular self and the outside world are unlikely alone to be sufficient to explain the origins of consciousness:

> the mechanisms underlying the "irritability" [the ability to respond to external stimuli] of protozoa are known to be the same as those involved in the hyper-sensitivity of all three main types of excitable cell in metazoan organisms (animals) – that is, sensory receptor cells, neurons, and muscle cells. These mechanisms are essentially the opening and closing of certain pores that allow some ions to pass freely across the cell membrane. Parsimony suggests that the sudden onslaught of positively-charged ions (cations) into the alkaline cytoplasm – the very definition of membrane excitability – is the key phenomenon involved in a cell's "awareness" of its environment ("sentience"). In other words, what makes cells with excitable membranes so unusual is their response to electrostatic disturbances of homeostasis (slight acidification of the normally alkaline cellular interior) following external stimulation. In order to produce the higher-level "awareness" of animal organisms, the activity of these numerous excitable cells to achieve a kind of sentience must be synchronized (in ways yet to be determined) for coherent organism-level behavior.

Koch is quick to retort:

> I fully concur with your sentiment that the influx of cations is of vital importance in cellular excitability. Without this, we would not be conscious. Of course, we also would not be conscious without a beating heart, adequate oxygenated blood-flow, an appropriate cocktail of neuromodulatory chemicals suffusing various brain regions, such as the cortico-thalamic system, and so on. These are all background conditions that enable consciousness to occur but they are by themselves insufficient. More is needed.

What this "more" consists of, Koch does not say. However, in his reply he takes his leave with an interesting aside:

> Finally, it is quite a different question whether single cell-organisms, worms or other simple metazoans – vastly simpler than mammals with their large brains – have sentience. I do share with the letter writers a hunch that it may well be that "it feels like something to be a worm." However, that is a question that right now can't be answered in any meaningful empirically accessible manner.

Koch is right that we cannot say anything at the moment about what it feels like to be a worm. But we can try to reason about the minimum conditions that must have underpinned the need to *feel like being* something, a worm or any other entity.

I think Damasio and colleagues hit on an important point by emphasising the role of the excitability properties of cell membranes. Ultimately, the important events, as we have seen, take place on the border, at the edges. It is there that the most enigmatic process of some biological systems actually occurs: that of an interior actively defining itself against an exterior: consciousness. But when does it become necessary to actively define an interior compared to an exterior? And why?

In a nutshell, the idea promoted by Damasio, Sacks and colleagues is that when animal cells open and close to the outside world, through the inflow and outflow of ions, they are doing more than just responding to external stimuli. According to these scholars, the inflow and outflow of ions could be the basis of consciousness. But the problem is that, as they themselves recognise, ion influx already causes simple movements of flagella and pseudopods in protozoa in response to external stimuli. These movements are determined by changes in ion concentrations in the cytoplasm. So why should these creatures be sentient about the stimulus that arrives at their boundary, given that they can respond appropriately to it without any explicit distinction between what is outside and what is inside that boundary? In other words, when (and why) does the distinction between "self" and "non-self" become necessary for an organism?

### Note

1 N. D. Cook, A. Damasio, G. B. Carvalho, H. T. Hunt and O. Sacks (2015), "An open letter to Christof Koch and C. Koch, A response to Cook and colleagues from Christof Koch". *Scientific American*, 17 June 2015.

# 12

# THE SCENT OF THE ROSE

Reid therefore distinguished perception from sensation,
saying that that was passive and did not administer ideas at all;
and that this active, and consisted of spontaneous and natural judgement
by which one acquires the persuasion of the existence of external bodies.
Antonio Rosmini

In recent years, numerous prestigious scholars have addressed the subject of consciousness, but I must confess the only one that caught my imagination was the evolutionary psychologist Nicholas Humphrey (whom we met previously for his hypothesis on the social function of intelligence, p. 9).[1]

In the beginning, Humphrey notes, being sensitive meant having local reactivity, that is, being able to produce a response limited to the site of stimulation, such as a wrinkling of the membrane in response to a noxious stimulus. A kind of representation, therefore, of what happens at the surface of the organism, i.e. what happens *to* it, to the organism itself.

Homeostatically modifying one's bodily state must have been important in the origin of minds. Light reaching the membrane burns: the membrane either shrivels to defend itself or, which is the same thing, becomes reddened. In both cases, the organism reacts to the stimulus with a change in bodily state. The stimulus, however, is not just something that arrives on the membrane to which it is fitting to react locally. It can be a sign of something out there, of something that is outside the boundaries of one's own body and not simply "on" one's body, i.e. on one's boundary. Thus, light or a shadow on the surface of the membrane is not merely a stimulus that – on the border between self and non-self – influences the animal's bodily state,

DOI: 10.4324/9781003491033-13

modifying its homeostasis. It is a signal that there is sun out there, or food, or a predator...

This idea that there are two different ways of representing stimuli, sensations, of representing *what* happens to me, and *perceptions*, what happens out there, is an idea that Humphrey borrows from Thomas Reid (1710–1796), the philosopher of the so-called "Scottish School". Reid writes in his *Essay on the Intellectual Powers of Man* (1785, cited in Humphrey 1992: 42[2]):

> The external senses have a double province – to make us feel, and to make us perceive. They furnish us with a variety of sensations, some pleasant, some painful, and others indifferent; at the same time, they give us a conception of and an irresistible belief in the existence of external objects. This conception of external objects is the work of nature; so likewise is the sensation that accompanies it. This conception and belief that nature produces by means of the senses, we call *perception*. The feeling that goes along with perception, we call *sensation*... Perception [by contrast] has always an external object; and the object of my perception, in this case, is that quality of the rose which I discern by the sense of smell.

The reason Reid emphasises the distinction between these two modes of representation is that sensation in itself does not imply the conception of external objects. Reid is concerned with the sceptical conclusions derived from David Hume's philosophy, according to which empirical knowledge can never tell us anything certain about the existence of external objects, such knowledge being based on contingent sensations. But for Reid, the external senses exercise a dual function: they make us feel, but they also make us *perceive* external objects. He uses the example of the scent of the rose to clarify his hypothesis. The scent of the rose that we can smell for its own sake, without any reference to the rose-object, constitutes sensation. It exists as long as someone can smell it. As Bishop Berkeley would say, its being consists in being perceived. But the smell of the rose also arouses in us the recognition of the external object; that is, the smell acts as a signal of one of the qualities of the external object. The correlation with the object can easily be verified, because if I move that specific rose, that specific object, away from me, its fragrance will become increasingly faint until it disappears altogether. As Reid claims, all this would solve the scandal represented by Hume's scepticism, according to which – since we trade in sensations alone – we can know nothing about external objects. In actual fact, Reid argues, the smell of the rose inhabits a dual province: that of the mind, as a sensation, but also that of the physical object, the rose, thus restoring the primacy of common sense, for which the scent of the rose is *in* the rose, not just in our sensation.

In the circumstances of ordinary life, the distinction between sensation and perception may appear vague, because our attention is usually directed to external objects rather than our sensations.[3] Fundamental to sensation, however, is its hedonic character, which according to Reid and Humphrey, derives from its motor origin: stimuli that reach the surface of the organism – its boundaries – are either pleasant or unpleasant, and the organism reacts with an appropriate response. Is the light hot? As a defensive manoeuvre, the membrane wrinkles or reddens. Does it smell good? The orifice that allows gases in the air to penetrate opens to receive it.

Primitive organisms possessed sensitivity to stimuli (such as light, mechanical vibrations or the level of salinity of water) spread over the entire surface of the body. These were not yet specialised receptors, but cilia that probably had both a sensory and a motor function. For example, photoreceptors, which respond to light, are thought to have originally been cilia with a tactile function, and it was only later that a photosensitive molecule joined these cilia, making them light-excitable, i.e. sensitive to the "touch" of light.

Even today, animals that possess light-sensitive structures spread over the body surface, such as earthworms, react to light stimulation as something happening *on* the body surface. If you dig up an earthworm, bringing it partially into the light, with its receptors, it will compare the area of its body that is illuminated with the area that is in the shade, so as to decide in which direction to move away from the light. The stimulation produced by light on the membrane seems to be something earthworms avoid.

In ancestral organisms that possessed only a diffuse sensitivity to light, this caused a bodily reaction that reflected the affective tone of the stimulus, but light was not yet a signal of "something out there" – it was only something that happened to the animal, at its boundaries.

However, we know that from the original undifferentiated response to light, the ability to respond to the direction of light evolved to form images. Today, light falling onto the camera eye of a human being or the compound eye of a bee is both something that happens to the organism (a sensation, i.e. a bodily reaction that reflects the hedonic value of the stimulus: I am approaching/moving away) and the signal of an object out there, along with its properties (How big is it? How close is it? How bright is it?).

It is not simply a development in the stages of information processing, with perception following on from sensation. Were this the case, it would not be possible to have perception in the absence of sensation. Humphrey was among the first researchers to demonstrate that the two representational modes run in parallel and not one behind the other, and that the emergence of perception did not lead to the abandonment of the older representational channel: sensation. This is clearly manifested in the phenomenon of "blindsight".

The facts are well known in clinical terms. Patients with lesions localised to the primary visual cortex present a region of the visual field that is blind, called the scotoma. When a stimulus, such as a flash of light, is projected onto the scotoma, e.g. in the upper or lower part, patients deny experiencing anything; that is, they deny having any sensation. However, if they are asked to guess the position of the flash, e.g. to say whether it is at the top or at the bottom, by pointing at it with their finger, although reluctant to answer and still denying that they see anything, they manage to give the correct answer very close to 100 per cent of the time. So they perceive something *out there* without experiencing anything *happening to them*.

The origin and initial inspiration for these observations are little known. Before the phenomenon reached the clinic, in fact, Humphrey had investigated the recovery of functions in a monkey, Helen, whose visual cortex had been surgically removed for experimental purposes.[4] After a few years, the animal, which was theoretically supposed to be "cortically blind", showed signs of an astonishing recovery, moving at ease in the environment without bumping into objects, in a manner indistinguishable in appearance from that of a seeing animal. A recovery,[5] however, that had strange aspects, as if Helen was unaware of her newfound abilities. Here is how Humphrey describes the situation:

> [S]he (Helen) no longer knew how that information come to her: if there was a currant before her eyes she would find that she knew its position but, lacking visual sensation, she no longer *saw* it as being there… The information she obtained through her eyes was "pure perceptual knowledge" for which she was aware and not substantiating evidence in the form of visual sensations. Helen "just knew" that there was a currant in such-and-such a position on the floor… "Blindsight" is what I think Helen had… The human patient, not surprisingly, believes that he is merely "guessing". What, after all, is a "guess"? It is defined in Chambers Dictionary as a "judgement or opinion without sufficient evidence or grounds".

Blindsight is thus characterised as a perception that is not accompanied by conscious sensation. The reverse situation, that of the absence of perception with the presence instead of an intact sensation, can be observed in another neurological condition: that of agnosia. In these circumstances, an inability on the part of patients to recognise objects, people, sounds and shapes that are already known is noted. All this in the absence of disturbances of memory or the sense organ involved. It is a kind of mental blindness, whereby the patient, as in the famous case described by Oliver Sacks, might mistake his wife for a hat (although recognition of one's spouse usually remains possible using some other sensory medium).

What is interesting is that agnostic patients do not find anything strange in their experiences, which are in fact in no way impaired in terms of sensation, but only in terms of perception.

## Notes

1 Humphrey gave a memorable lecture at the institute where I work; I have a vivid memory of a PhD student approaching him after the talk to ask him, visibly moved, "But when will we ever hear about consciousness from someone like you again?" And Nicholas replying politely: "You might be the one to give the next talk on consciousness."

2 N. Humphrey (1992), *A History of the Mind*. Chatto & Windus 1992, Simon & Schuster 1992; N. Humphrey (2006), *Seeing Red: A Study in Consciousness*. Belknap Press/Harvard University Press; N. Humphrey (2011), *Soul Dust: The Magic of Consciousness*. Quercus Publishing, Princeton University Press.

3 It can of course be argued that these properties are also phenomenal, for we access them through the functioning of our sense organs and nervous system. However, they are blatantly shared: not only the passage of our fingers, but also the flight of a butterfly is prevented by the presence of a surface such as a concrete wall. This seems evidence enough of the reality of the outside world, of its being imperturbable to our theories, motives and desires. And anyone who objects that after all, the butterfly and the wall are also phenomenal should try making their phenomenal butterfly pass through the phenomenal concrete wall. It seems that no idealist has ever succeeded. Of course, the fact that the phenomenal world is constrained does not imply that it truthfully reflects the constraints of the real world. There are arguments suggesting our perceptions are a bit like species-specific user interfaces, directing behaviour for survival and reproduction, not truth-seeking (https://www.quantamagazine.org/th e-evolutionary-argument-against-reality-20160421/; see also G. Vallortigara (2018), "Qui riposa l'etologo che parlò alle zecche" [Here rests the ethologist who spoke to the ticks]. *Il Domenicale, Sole 24 ore*, p. 17).

4 N. Humphrey and L. Weiskrantz (1967), "Vision in monkeys after removal of the striate cortex". *Nature*, 215: 595–597. A video of Helen's behaviour can be seen at: https://www.youtube.com/watch?v=6ek2LBqM7dk.

5 Partial recovery because, for example, Helen never recovered the ability to discriminate shapes and colours. However, a limited ability to discriminate shapes has also been observed in some patients with blindsight. See L. Weiskrantz (1986), *Blindsight: A Case Study and Implications*. Oxford University Press, Oxford, UK. The quotation of Humphrey is from N. Humphrey (1992), *A History of the Mind*. Chatto and Windus, London.

# 13

## *PRIMUM MOVENS*

I stepped from plank to plank
So slow and cautiously;
The stars about my head I felt,
About my feet the sea.

I knew not but the next
Would be my final inch, –
This gave me that precarious gait
Some call experience.

Emily Dickinson

When is it necessary to "feel" that something is happening on the surface of the body? Feeling is different from showing an appropriate bodily reaction. Let us go back to the origins, to organisms equipped with cilia in which the arrival of sensory stimulation resulted in a bodily reaction: the stimulus is harmful, I move away; the stimulus is beneficial, I stay there or move closer... The whole thing can be chemically mediated by the influx of ions through the cell membrane. However, there seems to be no need to "feel" anything here, i.e. to actively make a distinction between self and outside self. The distinction is somewhat implicit in the bodily response, but it is not yet a feeling. In fact, I can receive information on the surface of the body and respond to it appropriately without needing to feel anything. If sensation is a bodily response, as Humphrey believes, why is it that in some cases one can respond appropriately without "feeling" anything?

Humphrey argued that in primitive animals the response to stimulation remains locally confined: the organism encountering the noxious substance following membrane stimulation, via ion influx, produces a local contraction

DOI: 10.4324/9781003491033-14

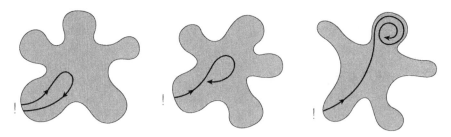

**FIGURE 13.1** Stages in the mental representation of stimulation according to Humphrey (see text). Originally, the stimulation produces a localised bodily response, right where the stimulus arrives (figure on the left); subsequently, the representation of what happens at the surface of the body is obtained by sending a command for the bodily response, but without executing the response itself, by privatising it (figure in the centre and on the right). The central part of the figure, however, reveals the problem that provides the starting point for the hypothesis presented in this book: the impossibility of distinguishing when a local response is produced by an external stimulation and when it is produced by the animal itself.

*Source:* Modified from Humphrey, N. (1994), "The private world of consciousness". *New Scientist*, 8 January 1994, pp. 23–25.

that mediates the "affective" response to the stimulus. In more developed animals, signals may come and go from a central ganglion, as schematised in Figure 13.1, but would still retain vestiges of the initial mechanism: that of the local body reaction.

However, the development of the perceptual channel may have played a role in the emergence of conscious sensations, even though perception in itself does not require being conscious. Humphrey comes close to solving the problem, in my opinion, when he observes that the only way to determine whether a part of our body is *ours* is to move it. For it is only with active movement that it becomes important to distinguish what is out there from what is happening on the surface of the body so as not to confuse them; it is at this point that what happens "to me" can become "feeling".

Neurobiologist Rodolfo Llinás drew attention to the fact that the brain evolved for active movement with a well-known example.[1] Ascidians are animals that live anchored to rocks or the seabed; they have a globular appearance and a pinkish or sometimes red colour, covered in a tunic – hence the name tunicates – made of a cellulose-like substance. They are filter feeders, meaning that their diet is based on microorganisms and particles in the water. The water is sucked in through an inhaling siphon and then expelled to the outside through an exhaling siphon, while the particles and micro-organisms remain imprisoned in the mucus and conveyed to the stomach.

Like other sessile organisms, adult ascidians have no true nervous system other than the few neurons needed to control filtering activity (inhalation and expulsion of water). Ascidian larvae, however, before the metamorphosis that will see them clinging to a fixed substrate, swim freely in the water, moving actively with their muscular tails. At this stage, in addition to a tail, the larva is equipped with a notochord: a flexible tube-like structure that runs the length of the body from head to tail and that is observed in all chordate embryos (which are named after it). The larvae survive a few days, sometimes only a few minutes, because as soon as they move they find a suitable substrate and anchor themselves to it, thanks to adhesive papillae located on the head. During metamorphosis following adhesion, the notochord and a large part of the nervous system, composed of around 300 neurons grouped in a ganglion in the head region, are reabsorbed and disappear.

The primitive brain of the ascidian larvae is capable of receiving and processing sensory information from the environment, either through statocysts – receptors that are stimulated by means of small mineral concretions (the statoliths), which shift with the movement associated with gravity, signalling to the organism its location in space – or through a local grouping of skin cells that are sensitive to light, a kind of primitive eye. This information-processing system ceases to be of any use once a convenient substrate to adhere to has been found, when the animal becomes sessile. The story has been read as a mischievous metaphor for the fate of the university professor, who, having obtained much-coveted tenure, like the ascidian, may attach himself firmly to the long sought-after substrate and dispose of his brain, which is now no longer needed.

That the substrate-attached ascidian digests its brain shows how it evolved to allow movement, not to immerse itself in elucubrations. It could therefore be argued that only when there is active movement does it become important to use the changes that stimuli induce locally, on the membrane surface, as a signal that there is something out there. In the absence of active movement, one can only react to what is happening on the membrane; whereas in the presence of active movement, one can develop sensorimotor stages in which the local change in stimulation is monitored step by step.

The simple bodily reaction does not in itself require perception as distinct from sensation. The reaction can be represented, for example, by the direct activity of the cilia, when this type of structure acted at the same time as a receptive and propulsive mechanism. The type of active movement we are discussing is in fact unlike that observed in unicellular animals that move by means of their cilia.

Consider, for example, how a paramecium moves in response to a noxious stimulus. The strategy is a bit like that of the bumper cars at the amusement park: after hitting something, you backtrack a little, turn the wheels and start again; if the coast is still not clear, you repeat the operation, backtrack,

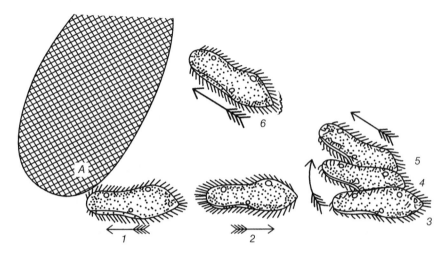

**FIGURE 13.2** The movement of a unicellular organism such as the paramecium is related to the variation in direction in which the cilia move in response to the entry of ions through the membranes when, for example, the animal encounters an area of different chemical composition (A) that induces avoidance.

*Source:* Adapted from Goodenough, J. McGuire, B. and Wallace, R. (1993). *Perspectives on Animal Behaviour.* Wiley, New York.

turn a little again and start again... Similarly, when it encounters a chemically unsuitable area, the paramecium moves backwards for a distance equal to a couple of times the length of its body, turns a little and then starts moving forwards again (this single-celled organism follows a spiral trajectory, rotating on its major axis, and when it encounters the obstacle it moves backwards diagonally to start off again in a new direction). The propulsive movement, forwards or backwards, depends on the direction in which the cilia that cover its body push, like little oars: forwards when the cilia push is directed towards the rear end of the animal, backwards when directed towards the front end (Figure 13.2). What determines the direction of the pushing is the concentration of calcium ions within the cilia: if it is low, the cilia push towards the posterior portion; if it is high, towards the anterior portion.[2] Thus, when the animal encounters a chemically noxious area, the permeability of the membrane to calcium ions changes, allowing the ions to enter and the cilia to push towards the posterior end, which causes the animal to move backwards. An ion pump, however, immediately sets to work to flush out the excess calcium ions and re-establish homeostatic equilibrium: a matter of a couple of seconds, the calcium ion concentration lowers again, the cilia begin to push towards the posterior end and the animal starts to move forward again. Here, it is clear, the movement is not active, because at all times its implementation depends on external circumstances: the influx of calcium ions caused by a change in membrane permeability on encountering the stimulus.

Returning to the question at hand: when (and why) does the distinction between "self" and "non-self" become necessary for an organism? It is necessary when the organism is moving actively, with some form of locomotion mediated by cells separate from those responsible for receiving stimuli. This is because when the organism is actively moving, it becomes essential to distinguish the sensory signals that come from the world outside from those that are the consequence of the organism's own movements in the world. Then, and only then, must the organism explicitly distinguish between self and non-self: between the things that happen to it and the things that it makes happen. What we call sentient is an organism that must, first of all, distinguish between the signals it generates itself and those that are generated on its membranes by all that is other than itself.

In order to have the kind of active movement that makes it possible for stimulation to "feel", it is necessary to have a distinct receptor system acting on a distinct motor system. In short, you need neurons and muscles.

## Notes

1 R. Llinás (2001), *I of the Vortex: From Neurons to Self*. MIT Press, Cambridge, Mass. On ascidians, see also A. Karaiskou, B. J. Swalla, Y. Sasakura and J. P. Chambon (2015), "Metamorphosis in solitary ascidians". *Genesis*, 53: 34–47; Y. Sasakura, K. Mita, Y. Ogura and T. Horie (2012), "Ascidians as excellent chordate models for studying the development of the nervous system during embryogenesis and metamorphosis". *Development, Growth & Differentiation*, 54: 420–437.
2 R. Eckert (1972), "Bioelectric control of ciliary activity". *Science*, 176: 473–481.

# 14

# EARLY ANIMALS, EARLY NEURONS

Say: how in the dark did you distinguish the bones?
the nerves stretched over the joints?
so many various textures
of veins, arteries and muscles didst thou form?
The viscera, fibres and ligaments?
How the guts did bend, tighten and swell?
How, with red flesh
clothing the whole, did you strip the head?
How did the heart obey? how did you halt it?

Tommaso Campanella

The origins of the nervous system are far from clear. Sponges do not possess neurons, but cells can communicate with each other via the influx of calcium ions that can mediate a contraction response in the entire body. However, it seems that the first animals to appear on Earth were not sponges, but ctenophores: gelatinous organisms that resemble jellyfish, but actually belong to a different taxonomic group.

Pluricellular animals (or metazoans in biologists' jargon) are divided into five groups: porifera (sponges); placozoans (vaguely resembling amoebae, and of which only one species has been described); cnidarians (jellyfish, corals); ctenophores – mentioned above; and bilaterians (all animals with bilateral symmetry, which account for 99 per cent of living species, including arthropods and vertebrates).

Porifera and placozoa do not possess neurons and muscles, at least in any recognisable form. Curiously, however, ctenophores do possess both neurons and muscles (and the mesoderm from which the muscles develop).

DOI: 10.4324/9781003491033-15

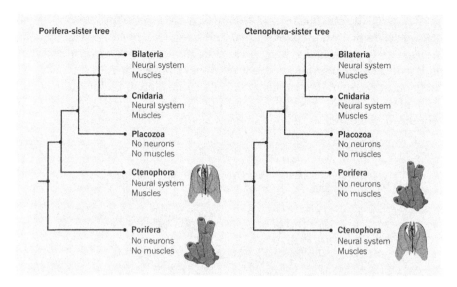

**FIGURE 14.1**    Two different hypotheses on the original branching of the animal kingdom: according to one hypothesis (left), sponges (porifera) would be the simplest group because they do not have neurons and muscles; according to an alternative hypothesis (right), based on genetic analysis, sponges would in fact appear to be phylogenetically closer to bilaterians and cnidarians than to ctenophores.

*Source:* Telford, M., Moroz, L. and Halanych, K. A. (2016), "Sisterly dispute". *Nature* 529, 286–287, doi:10.1038/529286a.

Traditionally, partly due to the fact that they lack both neurons and muscles, porifera have been regarded as deriving independently from the ancestral metazoans, i.e. as the divergent group of other animals (see the left-hand side of Figure 14.1). However, recent genetic analyses suggest that, despite possessing advanced features such as neurons and muscles, ctenophores may in fact be the divergent group.[1]

This leaves two possibilities open: that of a separate and independent evolution of nervous systems, which would have occurred at least twice over the course of evolution, in ctenophores and the common ancestor of cnidarians and bilaterians, or that of a later loss of neurons and muscles in placozoans and porifera (Figure 14.1).

That sponges may have possessed and then lost nerve-like cells is suggested by the fact that at the larval stage, these animals display stimulus-orientation behaviours such as phototaxy and the presence of light-sensitive cells. Furthermore, although sponges are not actually endowed with nerve cells, they possess numerous genes that – in bilaterians and cnidarians – are associated with the presence of nerve cells.

Whatever the outcome of the dispute over the relative precedence of porifera or ctenophores, it seems clear that even in the absence of true synaptic transmission, the cells in sponges can communicate with each other by the influx of calcium ions[2] and in this way convey simple activities such as a contraction response of the whole organism, i.e. the kind of bodily reaction that Humphrey imagines was the origin of the sensation (as in *A* in Figure 14.2). But this does not tell us that the sponges have to "feel" something when they

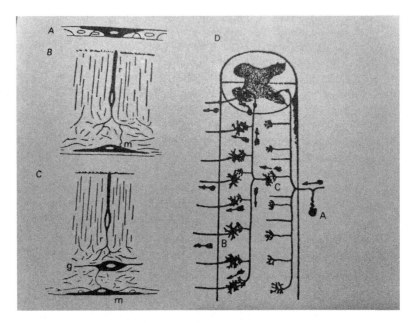

**FIGURE 14.2**  Rodolfo Llinás' reconstruction of some crucial stages in the evolution of nervous systems. In *A*, in black a cell that enables motility in animals such as sponges: stimulation causes a contraction wave; in *B* the two functions, contractile and sensory, are segregated, with the appearance of a distinct sensory cell and muscle cell: at this stage, represented by e.g. sea anemones, the sensory cell also acts as a motor neuron because it stimulates the muscle cell; in *C*, a second neuron is interposed between the sensory neuron and the muscle fibre, with the function of activating the muscle: a motor neuron that responds only to the activation of the sensory cell (again in a sea anemone); the next step, in *D*, is that of the interposition of an interneuron between the sensory neuron and the motor neuron (the example here is related to the vertebrate spinal cord). The branching of the interneuron allows it to transfer information from the sensory neuron to many other neurons, both motor and other interneurons.

*Source:* Llinás, R. (2001), *I of the Vortex: From Neurons to Self.* MIT Press, Cambridge, Mass.

contract: in fact, they could contract in an appropriate way at the onset of the stimulus without needing to feel anything.

A crucial step must have been to have neurons (B in Figure 14.2) such as a sensory neuron that receives a signal on the body surface and passes it on to a motor neuron that makes a muscle act. There is no single genetic marker of neurons – a large proportion of the genes that oversee the production of neurons are also expressed in other cell types – and there are no specific genes expressed in all types of neurons. The only possible definition of a neuron is therefore a functional one: a cell dedicated to electrical communication that addresses other discrete and distant cellular elements using synapses and the (pre- and post-synaptic) elements attached to them. Electrical communication mediated by the potential of action affords greater speed of response, and this applies to both the sensory reception part and the muscular action part.

For muscles, too, the transition must have been progressive, and may have occurred several times throughout evolutionary history. Sponges do not have muscles but myosin, the protein that gives animal muscles their striated appearance, and that plays a crucial role in regulating water flow and cell motility. Cnidarians, on the other hand, which do possess striated muscles, appear to have developed them independently of bilaterians.

Muscles and neurons enable locomotion and thus much more articulate behaviour in animals. But this in itself does not justify "feeling" something when the surface is stimulated. It makes little difference whether the response is a general bodily contraction, as in a sponge or an amoeba, or whether it is the specific contraction of a muscle produced by the action potential of a motor neuron, which in turn is stimulated by the sensory neuron that has transduced the stimulation arriving at the surface of the membrane (e.g. a light stimulus) into an electrical signal. Yet we still do not see the *reason why* behind a sensation.

### Notes

1 J. F. Ryan and M. Chiodin (2015), "Where is my mind? How sponges and placozoans may have lost neural cell types". *Philosophical Transactions of the Royal Society of London B*, 370: 20150059, doi:10.1098/rstb.2015.0059.
2 The action potential, which underlies neuronal functioning, first appeared in unicellular eukaryotic organisms, but using the calcium potential instead of the sodium potential, and it is thought that the mechanism was later adapted in multicellular animals.

# 15

# THE CROOKED-HEADED FLY

*Eristalis* flies are a genus of dipterans, belonging to the hoverfly family. You will probably have come across one of the most common species of the family, *Eristalis tenax*, also known as the "drone fly", and perhaps confused it with a bee because of their similarity in appearance (Figure 15.1).

The *Eristalis* has a thin, mobile neck, which makes it possible to gently rotate its head 180 degrees around its longitudinal axis and glue it to the thorax. The result of such an operation is that the right eye will occupy the

**FIGURE 15.1**   A hoverfly (Eristalis tenax).

*Source:* Sharp Photography via Wikimedia Commons.

DOI: 10.4324/9781003491033-16

position of the left and vice versa.[1] The experiment was described in 1950 by Erich von Holst and his then student Horst Mittelstaedt. The aim was to clarify the dynamic processes that regulate the relationship between the impulses arriving at the nervous system via the sense organs (known as *afference*) and those that are transmitted, either directly or indirectly, to the periphery, i.e. the muscles (known as *efference*).

Erich von Holst (1908–1962) is a little-known figure compared with Konrad Lorenz, but one who profoundly influenced the study of ethology and behavioural physiology (Figure 15.2). Due to a severe and incurable heart defect, caused by a form of rheumatoid arthritis contracted in his youth, von Holst grew up with the acute awareness that his life would soon come to an end (he died at only 54 years of age), and for this reason he developed a personality and style marked by indefatigability and inflexibility.

**FIGURE 15.2**   Konrad Lorenz (left) and Erich von Holst (right) at the Max Planck Institute for Behavioural Physiology in Seewiesen, Germany, 1958.

He can't have been an easy man to get along with. His students could call on him at any time of day or night for anything to do with experiments and science, but he demanded the same dedication from them. Few could lay claim to such prodigious energy, which led him to range from the physiology of the nervous system to the construction of flying mechanical birds, to the making of asymmetrically shaped viols to facilitate their use by musicians (he was an excellent violist and, shortly before his death, had embarked on the writing of a popular book on the science of violins, which remained unfinished).[2]

In his autobiography, Lorenz recounts his first encounter with von Holst. During a lecture, the already-famous ethologist was trying to trace the phenomena of instinctive behaviour back to the traditional idea of the chain of reflexes, as laid out by the physiologist Sherrington. Lorenz writes:

> [M]y wife was sitting behind a young man who clearly agreed with what I was saying about spontaneity, murmuring to himself many times: "Yes, that makes sense." But when, at the end of my lecture, I said I nevertheless considered instinctive motor patterns to be chain reflexes, he buried his face in his hands and uttered despondently: "Idiot, idiot!" That man was Erich von Holst.[3]

Lorenz was soon convinced by von Holst that the reflex theory could not be sustained:

> The most important step forward in all our attempts to understand both animal and human behaviour is in my opinion the identification of this fact: the elementary nervous structure that underlies behaviour does not consist of a receptor, of an afferent neuron that stimulates a motor cell, and of an effector activated by the latter. Von Holst's hypothesis, which we can safely make our own, states that the basic central nervous organisation consists of a cell that is permanently characterized by an endogenous activity, yet which is prevented from affecting its effector by another cell, one which – also producing an endogenous activity – exerts an inhibitory effect. It is this inhibitory cell that is influenced by the receptor, and which ceases its inhibitory activity at the biologically "right" time.[4]

The hypothesis appeared so promising that, in order to investigate it further, the Max Planck Society set up an institute for the study of "Behavioural Physiology" in Seewiesen, Upper Bavaria, with von Holst as director and Lorenz as co-director. "I am convinced," Lorenz would later say in his Nobel speech, "that if he [von Holst] were still alive, he would be here in Stockholm now."[5]

Von Holst introduced a cybernetic approach to the study of ethology, being among the first to argue – in an era dominated by reflex theory and behaviourism – that behavioural phenomena cannot be explained as being caused by external stimuli but rather by regulation and self-regulation mechanisms. Animals do not react as empty shells shaped by environmental stimuli but as active systems that anticipate and predict the outcomes and consequences of environmental stimuli. This is precisely the case with the relationship between sensory afference and motor efference. Von Holst had guessed that the nervous instructions that reach the muscles and generate body movements must in some way be able to take into account the sensory effects produced by those same movements; i.e. they must be able to anticipate reafferent stimulation and implement the necessary adjustments.

With his student Mittelstaedt, von Holst placed the *Eristalis* fly in a cylinder with black-and-white vertical stripes.[6] When the cylinder began to rotate in a particular direction (Figure 15.3), the animal would start to move in the same direction, in an attempt to stabilise its visual world.

This optomotor response is well known, as we noted in connection with Reichardt's motion detector. However, on reflection, not everything is as simple as it appears.

When an object moves in a certain direction, the image shifts on the retina in the opposite direction if the eye stands still (as is the case with the *Eristalis* fly). Consider, however, the opposite situation, in which it is the fly that starts to move in a cylinder that instead remains still. The animal's eyes receive stimulation identical to that of the previous case. When the fly is stationary and the

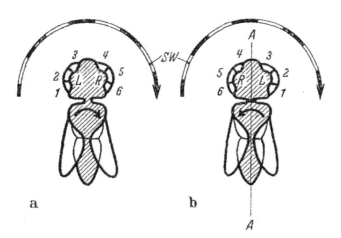

**FIGURE 15.3**   On the left (a), a normal *Eristalis* fly and, on the right (b), one with its head rotated 180 degrees along the longitudinal axis, placed inside a cylinder of which the walls are covered in black-and-white vertical stripes.

*Source:* E. Von Holst and H. Mittelstaedt (1950), "Das Reafferenzprinzip. Wechselwirkungen zwischen Zentralnervensystem und Peripherie" [The reafference principle. Interactions between the central nervous system and the periphery]. *Naturwissenschaften*, 27: 464–476.

cylinder is moving, say, clockwise, the image slides across the animal's retina anticlockwise. When, on the other hand, the cylinder is stationary and the fly is moving, again clockwise, the image slides across the animal's retina anticlockwise. But why in this second case does the optomotor response not come into action to bring the animal back to its initial state? The most obvious explanation is to assume that the optomotor reflex is inhibited during spontaneous locomotion. But the crooked-headed fly experiment shows this is not what happens.

When the fly's head is twisted (swivelling 180 degrees), the rotation of the cylinder – which we shall again assume to be clockwise – produces a sliding of the image on the retina identical to that caused by an anticlockwise rotation in an animal with its head in a normal position. The fly should therefore react to a rightward movement of the cylinder with a rotation of its body to the left, i.e. in the wrong direction considering its aim of stabilising its visual world. If, however, the animal is free to move and the cylinder is stationary, one would expect locomotion to be normal, as in the case of the unswivelled head, insofar as the optomotor response is inhibited. In actual fact, the crooked-headed fly cannot move normally in the cylinder. In the words of von Holst and Mittelstaedt: "the Eristalis continues to turn in tight circles to the left or right or shows short, pronounced turning movements to the right or left until it comes to a halt, as if frozen in an atypical posture".[7]

In short, when the head is straight, everything happens as if, by moving in the world, the fly "expects" a specific direction of image sliding on the retina, which would consequently be neutralised. Conversely, when the sliding of the image takes place in the opposite direction to that expected, due to the head swivelling around, the corrective movement has the opposite effect to neutralisation, because the sliding of the image in the direction opposite to that expected is increased. The process creates positive retroaction: the more the animal rotates to correct, the more the variation between expectation and perception increases. Thus, as soon as the fly starts a rotational movement in one direction, it is as if it is "optically pushed" in the same direction; if it tries to rotate in the opposite direction, the problem recurs. So the fly scurries back and forth for a while, twists and eventually comes to a halt, all snarled up... But if the head is unglued from the thorax, meaning it can rotate back to its canonical orientation, locomotion resumes normally.

It was at this point that von Holst and Mittelstaedt had an idea. Perhaps the behaviour of the Eristalis fly can be explained by imagining that every time an organism engages in an activity, a copy of the motor signal (the Efferenzkopie, i.e. efferent copy) is sent to the sensory system. In this way, the efferent copy can be used to compare the expected movement with the actual movement, creating a feedback system capable of stabilising the organism. A simple diagram of how this works can be seen in Figure 15.4, referring in this case to vision and eye movements in the human eye.

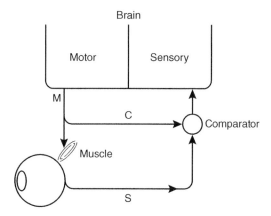

**FIGURE 15.4**   From the brain comes an efferent signal (motor, M) to the extra-ocular muscles that make the eyes move. An efferent copy (C, efferent copy or corollary discharge) of this signal is sent to the comparator, so that the afferent signal (sensory, S), which is produced as a result of the image scrolling on the retina, may be cancelled when it is produced – as in this case – by eye movement rather than the movement of an object in the outside world.

*Source:* Teuber, H-L. (1960), "Perception". In J. Field, H. W. Magoun and V. E. Hall (eds.), *Handbook of Physiology* (section 1, vol. 3). Washington DC, American Physiological Society.

Let us imagine that an object is moving in front of the eye. If the eye is motionless, the image will flow across the retina. Since in this case no movement signal is sent to the eye muscles, there will also be no efferent copy reaching the comparator and therefore movement will be perceived. In real life, however, the eyes do not stay still as they do when an *Eristalis* fly's head is glued to its body. Instead, they chase the object by means of movements controlled by the extra-ocular muscles, with the result that the image on the retina does not move. But why do we nevertheless see movement in this case? Because, together with the command to move the eye muscles, an efferent copy is sent to the comparator, which then receives a signal that we interpret as movement of the object.

A simple demonstration of the elegance of this explanation can be obtained by mechanically moving your eyeball passively, pushing it slightly from the outside with short finger presses. In this case, you will have the impression that the visual scene moves in jerks in correspondence to the pressure exerted on the eyeball. As this is a mechanical displacement of the eye from the outside, there is no signal from the brain to the muscles and therefore no efferent copy to the comparator either: in this case, the slipping of the image on the retina – not being cancelled by the efferent copy – is perceived.

The opposite effect occurs when a person with paralysed eye muscles (pharmacologically induced, for example) tries to shift their gaze: in this case the shift of the retinal image is missing, but since the brain has sent the command for the movement, the efferent copy of the motor command generates the rather unpleasant impression that the world is moving every time the person tries to move their eyes.

Over the same period that von Holst and Mittelstaedt were making *Eristalis* flies' heads turn, the psychobiologist Roger Sperry (1913–1994) was independently conducting similar experiments in the United States on fish, frogs and newts, surgically reversing the left–right or up–down position of the eyes. The results were the same as those observed by von Holst: a fish or frog with inverted eyes starts to turn in circles. Sperry introduced the use of the term "corollary discharge" to indicate the idea of an activity of motor origin that is copied to the sensory system.[8] This provides a clear analogy with von Holst and Mittelstaedt's notion of efferent copying.

The original thinking behind the problem and the authorship of the solution is actually even more complex.[9] The German physiologist Johann Georg Steinbuch (1770–1818), while studying how we actively recognise objects by touch, for example by grasping and exploring them with one hand, put forward the idea that there was an interaction between the efferent control mechanisms of hand movement, which he called *Bewegidee* (idea of movement), when the afferent sensory signals are evoked in the mechanoreceptors by touching the object. In particular, he pointed out that active hand movement could easily lead to object recognition, while the passive movement of stimulating the mechanoreceptors on the fingers and palm, even over a prolonged period of time, was not very or not at all effective.

The physicist and physiologist Hermann von Helmholtz (1821–1894) also got this far: he devised the example of the passive mechanical displacement of the eyeball compared with the active displacement produced by the extra-ocular muscles.[10] According to von Helmholtz, the fact that we see the world move in the first case but not in the second could be explained by imagining that when the eyeball is actively moved, an efferent copy of the command to move the extra-ocular muscle is sent to the sensory system.[11] However, Charles Sherrington (1857–1952), the founding father of neurophysiology, opposed this idea, arguing that muscles have their own sensitivity to the movements they produce (proprioceptive sensitivity). It was probably because of this opposition that the efferent-copy hypothesis did not gain momentum until after the work of von Holst and Sperry, almost 70 years later.

Of course, the concept of efferent copy/corollary discharge (or of the "reafference principle") has since undergone further development. The physicist and cybernetician Donald MacKay (1966) introduced the concept of "feedforward"[12] to better render the simple idea of signal cancellation in quantitative terms through the efferent copying hypothesised by von Holst and Mittelstaedt. In the feedforward control mechanism, the motor commands are monitored and evaluated before the efferent (e.g. the muscle controlling eye movement) takes action. In essence, this would appear to constitute an anticipatory control mechanism that would be largely carried out within the nervous system; in fact, having its origin within the nervous system itself, it might be better labelled "internal feedback", according to some scholars.[13]

You will have guessed by now why I am telling you all this. The story of the crooked-headed fly clarifies the problem that the development of locomotion entailed for animals: the need to discriminate between two varieties of stimulation, ones which are not distinguishable in terms of the effect they exert on the membranes, but only in terms of their origin. The way to determine their origin is through a circuit that re-sends the command of the bodily response to the system that must decide what is received. At this point, the stimulation on the membrane becomes an explicit "feeling" because now the organism must distinguish between what is happening to it and what is happening out there, i.e. it must actively represent itself in relation to its surroundings.

There is no need to make such a distinction, and thus to have sensations, as long as there is no room for misunderstanding. In fact, the story as told to us by Reid and Humphrey holds up very well even for a fissile organism: the organism responds (without feeling anything) with a global or local contraction of the body and, since it is not actively moving, it has no need to represent objects out there, because it has no way of intervening on such objects. As soon as it does – and a conception of "something out there" goes hand in hand with what happens on the surface of the body – then it must feel what difference it makes when something happens to itself (at the boundary between itself and outside itself) and when something happens out there.[14]

We might reconsider Steinbuch's experiment in this respect. Imagine that you move your finger until it encounters an obstacle. What do you feel at the moment of contact? You feel that there is something out there that you have encountered with your touch. However, you do not feel anything has happened to you unless you make an active effort to focus your attention on your finger rather than on the obstacle. But if you do the opposite and – with your eyes closed – ask someone to move an object until it runs up against your finger, the impression on the epidermis of your finger will be that of something that has happened to you. In the first case, the efferent copy has cancelled the sensation (what happens to you) making the presence of an external object objective. In the second case, the absence of the efferent copy leaves the "feeling" of something happening on the surface between self and non-self.

In the novel, *La vergine e i filosofi* [The virgin and the philosophers], by Valentino Braitenberg, a young woman named Ill approaches a stranger who is travelling with his antique violin, and together they set off on a journey in search of a theory of consciousness.[15] When they meet the director of the Con-Scientia Institute, a discussion ensues about where consciousness lies:

> The director broke off his speech and slid off the corner of the table to take a wooden rod from a shelf, perhaps a ruler. He handed it to Ill, inviting her to scratch the floor with it. It was made of rough travertine slabs, divided by grooves.
>
> "Close your eyes," he ordered, "and tell me what you perceive."
>
> "A rough stone," Ill said, "and a groove."
>
> "Where do you feel them?"
>
> "On the floor, of course," replied Ill somewhat incredulously.
>
> "And so your sensitivity would appear to lie on the tip of the rod, not in your brain? Or did you perhaps feel the roughness of the floor with your hand? Brain scholars teach us there are the nerves of sensitivity in there which transmit the sensation. But no, you perceived it in the rod and precisely on its lower tip."

This is the answer I would give. Seeing as she is actively moving the rod, Ill perceives the travertine surface with its properties and fissures as "out there". What happens to her, on the other hand, can be grasped as something distinct from the "persuasion of the existence of external bodies" as mentioned by the philosopher Antonio Rosmini (1797–1855): the tactile sensation caused by the rod on her palm and fingers.[16]

My argument is simply that before the evolution of the reafference circuit, the touch of an object on the surface of the body produced only the bodily reaction, and that only with the invention of the efferent copy – made necessary by active locomotion – did sensations begin to "be felt".[17]

The idea that *reafference*, i.e. that which is produced by the subject's own action rather than by *ex-afference*, by the objects out there, might provide a basis for the distinction between the self and non-self has seemed evident to numerous other scholars. The philosopher Peter Godfrey-Smith, for example, in his charming book on the octopus mind, traces the mechanism of efferent copying (or corollary discharge) to the idea of using actions to "feed" perceptions.[18] He mentions the neuroscientist Biorn Merker[19] in relation to the very possibility of animal action: a worm retracts when touched as a defensive manoeuvre; however, when it crawls through the ground it is continually touched – if it were to retract with every tactile stimulation, it would no longer be able to move forward!

The problem, however, is that if the efferent copy mechanism is not combined with the Reid–Humphrey distinction between sensation and perception, the emergence of experience cannot be explained. Perception, as we have noted, can be non-conscious, as in blind sight (and in Reid and Humphrey's idea, only sensation is conscious). So the fact that perception is influenced by action does not change things: the emergence of experience cannot be explained in this way. Instead, we must start from the acknowledgement that in the early days of minds, sensory stimulation produced a localised bodily reaction. And it is this bodily reaction – i.e. a kind of action – that has become sensation. Thus it is not simply an action that influences (or that "nourishes", in Godfrey-Smith's words) perception, but rather the fact that what was originally a mere reaction on the bodily surface – an acceptance of or withdrawal from stimulation – at the moment it is necessary to distinguish whether this reaction is produced by the stimulation itself or by the animal becomes something that is "felt" in the former case but not in the latter. In short, the efferent copying mechanism can by its own operation provide the minimum conditions for the stimulation to be either "felt" or "perceived".

Circulating since the dawn of cybernetics is the intuition that consciousness must have something to do with retroaction.[20] However, like Reid and Humphrey, I believe the emergence of consciousness is first and foremost linked to the very possibility of sensation as distinct from perception, which is made possible by exploiting the retroactive mechanism. It is important to emphasise this because there is nothing magical about the feedforward mechanism per se, as it also has a variety of applications outside the biological world. Nevertheless, one issue remains, and it requires further examination.

The idea of efferent copy or corollary discharge is a good explanation for why sensation is, so to speak, put on the back burner when one actively moves a finger and moves up to an object, or when moving a stick, as Ill does, one senses the travertine on the tip of the stick. However, why should one feel something when there is *no* corollary discharge? That is, when the sensory signal escapes from the comparator undisturbed? The sensory signal manifested itself even before there was a comparator and a corollary discharge. Why should it be felt now and not before? My impression is that the pieces of the puzzle have been in front of us for quite some time: they just need to be arranged correctly. We have to find a way to make Erich von Holst's fly land on Thomas Reid's rose.

## Notes

1 So, in actual fact, the head is reversed or swivelled rather than crooked, but "crooked-headed" sounds better in the title and refers here – etymologically – to the idea of twisting (i.e. crooked in the sense of being twisted around).

2 The book was supposed to be called *Geigenkunde für Liebhaber* [Violin science for amateurs]. Among von Holst's other passions was that for bird flight, which he attempted to reproduce using mechanical models. The best-known of his reconstructions is a pterosaur of the Mesozoic, the Rhamphorhynchus, which he apparently flew during a palaeontology conference. Several of von Holst's ornithopters may be admired in this historic footage: https://www.youtube.com/watch?v=VdrwOs9owuM.

3 "Konrad Lorenz – Biographical". NobelPrize.org. Nobel Prize Outreach AB 2024. https://www.nobelprize.org/prizes/medicine/1973/lorenz/biographical/.

4 "Konrad Lorenz – Biographical". NobelPrize.org. Nobel Prize Outreach AB 2024. https://www.nobelprize.org/prizes/medicine/1973/lorenz/biographical/.

5 "Konrad Lorenz – Biographical". NobelPrize.org. Nobel Prize Outreach AB 2024. https://www.nobelprize.org/prizes/medicine/1973/lorenz/biographical/.

6 E. Von Holst and H. Mittelstaedt (1950), "Das Reafferenzprinzip. Wechselwirkungen zwischen Zentralnervensystem und Peripherie" [The reafference principle. Interactions between the central nervous system and the periphery]. *Naturwissenschaften*, 27: 464–476. For an English translation of von Holst's main works, see: *The Behavioural Physiology of Animal and Man: The Collected Papers of Erich von Holst*, vol. 1, Methuen, London (1973) (translated by R. Martin). It is curious that, despite often being mentioned in neuroscience textbooks (usually in the chapter on perception), von Holst's experiment and its broad implications have been little publicised; a notable exception is the volume by A. Ananthaswamy (2015), *The Man Who Wasn't There*. Dutton, New York.

7 E. Von Holst and H. Mittelstaedt (1950), "Das Reafferenzprinzip. Wechselwirkungen zwischen Zentralnervensystem und Peripherie" [The reafference principle. Interactions between the central nervous system and the periphery]. *Naturwissenschaften*, 27: 464–476.

8 R. W. Sperry (1950), "Neural basis of the spontaneous optokinetic response produced by visual inversion". *Journal of Comparative and Physiological Psychology*, 43: 482–489.

9 For a historical reconstruction, by way of example see O.-J. Grüsser (1995), "On the history of the ideas of efference copy and reafference". In Claude Debru, *Essays in the History of Physiological Sciences: Proceedings of a Symposium Held at the University Louis Pasteur Strasbourg, on March 26–27th, 1993*. The Wellcome Institute Series in the History of Medicine: *Clio Medica*, 33, pp. 35–56.

10 Actually, it seems that von Helmholtz's explanation was not entirely correct. If people press on the eyeball while keeping their gaze fixed on a particular point, their eyes move very little (see L. Stark and B. Bridgeman (1983), "Role of corollary discharge in space constancy". *Perception and Psychophysics*, 34: 371–380). This is probably due to the fact that, in order to maintain stable fixation, the eye muscles contract so as to counteract the pressure of the finger on the eyeball. It would therefore be this signal sent to the extra-ocular muscles to keep the eyeball in position that produces the corollary discharge, and this, in the absence of a sensory signal to cancel it, would lead to the impression of movement.

11 In an email exchange, the physicist-mathematician and visual perception theorist Jan Koenderink drew my attention to the fact that the biologist Jakob Johann von Uexküll (1864–1944) had also anticipated the notion of reafference, but was curiously ignored by von Holst and Mittelstaedt, perhaps because of accusations of vitalism levelled at him by Konrad Lorenz (1903–1989). (I alluded to this story when recounting von Uexküll's final years spent in Capri – see G. Vallortigara (2018), "Qui riposa l'etologo che parlò alle zecche". *Domenica Il Sole 24 Ore*, August 2018). In *Theoretical Biology* (Jakob von Uexküll, English edition translated by D. L. MacKinnon, London: Kegan Paul, Trench, Trubner & Co, 1926), there is a diagram (p. 157), not unlike that of von Holst's *Efferenzkopie*. The neurobiologist Kostya Anokhin mentioned to me that his grandfather, the renowned Russian physiologist Pyotr Anokhin, anticipated the idea of a role of the efference copy in consciousness. Anokhin, K. (2021). Cognitom: In search of fundamental neuroscientific theory of consciousness. Zhurnal vysshei nervnoi deiatel'nosti 71(1): 39–71.

12 D. M. MacKay (1966), "Cerebral organization and the conscious control of action". In: J. C. Eccles (ed.), *Brain and Conscious Experience*. New York: Springer Verlag, pp. 422–445.

13 E. V. Evarts (1971), "Feedback and corollary discharge: A merging of the concepts". *Neurosciences Research Program Bulletin*, 9: 86–112.

14 In his more recent book, which is a delight to read, Humphrey adds the role of the efference copy, see p. 108 of: N. Humphrey (2022), *Sentience*. Oxford University Press, Oxford.

15 V. Braitenberg (2006), *La vergine e i filosofi* [The virgin and the philosophers]. Traven Books, Laives. The stranger travelling with his violin is clearly Valentino himself, who was a talented musician. Although this was his only novel, for a long time Braitenberg served as co-director of the Max-Planck Institute in Tübingen together with Reichardt, where he made important contributions to the study of the fly's visual system. For this purpose, he used the reaction the fly exhibits when it sees an approaching surface, thrusting its legs forwards and outwards in preparation for landing. To elicit the landing reaction under controlled conditions, Braitenberg placed the animal suspended in front of a rotating spiral; since the brightness and distance from the spiral were fixed, the fly showed the landing reaction only when the spiral's direction of rotation was such as to induce the sensation of an expansion of the surface, but not when rotating in the opposite direction, where the sensation was one of contraction. See V. Braitenberg and C. Taddei Ferretti (1966), "Landing reaction of *Musca Domestica* induced by visual stimuli". *Naturwissenschaften*, 53: 155.

16 For an original discussion on consciousness both inside and outside the head, see R. Manzotti (2017), *The Spread Mind. Why Consciousness and the World Are One*. OR Books, New York; and also the debate between Riccardo Manzotti and Tim Parks in the *New York Review of Books*, https://www.nybooks.com/topics/on-consciousness/ and the book by T. Parks (2018), *Out of My Head*. Penguin, Random House, London.

17 The connection in the opening citation between the *Eristalis* fly and the philosopher Antonio Rosmini is perhaps not obvious. In his "Nuovo saggio sull'origine delle idee" [New essay on the origin of ideas] (1830), Rosmini takes up Reid's distinction between perception and sensation and addresses the problem of the origin of knowledge. Sensation, which Rosmini terms "sensory perception", would appear to be nothing other than the perception of a modification that our body registers from a sensible object. But, according to Rosmini, this presupposes a previous sensation of the subject's own body, which he calls "fundamental bodily feeling". I understand the problem Rosmini poses, but it seems to me that the idea of the fundamental bodily feeling leads us to take a step backwards. Where is this primal "feeling" of the body supposed to come from? Rosmini states: "Sensations demand the immediate consciousness of our corporeity, of which they are nothing but modifications". But an immediate consciousness of our corporeity has no reason to exist if there is no circumstance in which it is necessary to distinguish whether the modifications that take place in it are produced by the body itself or by something external to it. Why else should one feel the body or feel anything at all? Only when an interior actively is defined in relation to an exterior is there any "feeling". I am grateful to Carlo Brentari for having introduced me in a most convivial manner to the thought of my fellow-citizen and philosopher. Carlo, as well as being Secretary in Rovereto of the Centro Studi Rosmini of the University of Trento, is one of the leading experts on the work of Jacob von Uexküll, who as we have noted was among the (unacknowledged) forerunners of the idea of efference copy (see footnote 8, above).

18 P. Godfrey-Smith (2016), *Other Minds. The Octopus and the Evolution of Intelligent Life*. HarperCollins Publishers, London.

19 B. Merker (2005), "The liabilities of mobility: A selection pressure for the transition to consciousness in animal evolution". *Consciousness and Cognition*, 14: 89–114. Merker, however, proposes a different idea from the one I present here. He argues that the worm can realise the reafference mechanism with a peripheral circuit, and that only in more complex animals does the problem of a centralised interface between the various senses and motor demands arise, with a centralised nervous system. This is because, for example, the receptors of the various sensory modalities are located differently on the body and are therefore affected in different ways by the body's movement in the environment. This in my view leads to an impasse, for Merker overlooks the fact that different sensations retain the specific contents of the sensory modality to which they belong. More generally, as noted by Umiltà, the implicit/explicit (unconscious/conscious) dissociations revealed by neuropsychology and experimental psychology are always domain-specific (see C. A. Umiltà (2000), "Conscious experience depends on multiple brain systems". *European Psychologist*, 5: 3–11). Patients with blind sight do not have blind hearing or blind touch, and in general, there has never been a patient described as a complete zombie, i.e. who behaved in all possible aspects in a normal manner in the absence of conscious experience (strictly speaking, it might potentially be that everyone is a zombie, with the exception of the author of these lines). This evidence flies in the face of the idea of a unitary, centralised area in the nervous system on which consciousness depends. The problem with hypotheses such as Merker's and Godfrey-Smith's is that they are still tied to the relationship between perception and action, whereas the crucial point, in my opinion, is that the reafference mechanism justifies and accounts for the distinction hypothesised by Reid between sensation and perception, between what happens to me and what happens *out there*.

20 For example, see R. Cordeschi, G. Tamburrini and G. Trautteur (1999), "The notion of loop in the study of consciousness". In *Neuronal Bases and Psychological Aspects of Consciousness*, C. Taddei-Ferretti and C. Musio (eds.), pp. 524–540. World Scientific, Singapore; D. Hofstadter (1979), *Gödel, Escher, Bach: An Eternal Golden Braid*. Basic Books, New York; and D. Hofstadter (2007), *I Am a Strange Loop*. Basic Books, New York.

# 16

## IMMINENCE OF A REVELATION

First of all, let's see where we have got to. Actively moving organisms must be able to distinguish in the stimuli that reach the sense organs those that are genuinely produced by external objects from those that are instead generated as a result of their own movement. When the latter is the case, sensory stimulation is, as it were, "explained away" by the efferent copy. However, if we remain confined to a generic relation between perception and action, we find ourselves at an impasse. The efferent copy cancels out perception when it is the result of active movement, but what happens when we perceive something instead? More precisely, when we "feel" something, for as we have already noted, one can perceive things just fine without feeling anything (p. 67).

One hypothesis is that time plays a crucial role, because in order to be able to make the comparison, the comparator must receive the two signals together, for example by delaying the one that arrives first, somewhat like in the Reichardt detector. This aspect of time delay is somewhat specific and inherent to the principle of reafference, in the sense that it could not be present – insofar as it had no reason to be – *before* its appearance.

The efferent copy anticipates the arrival of the sensory signal, so when the signal arrives and there is no efferent copy waiting for it, only the delay necessary for the operation of the comparator (for the operation of an interneuron, as we shall see in a moment) will be observed. This delay, the time required for the comparison of signals in the comparator, could account for the fact that sensation always has a minimum duration, even independently of sensory adaptation phenomena.[1]

On the other hand, when there is an efferent copy waiting for the sensory signal, it is inconceivable for the corollary motor signal to be delayed or kept in memory *ad infinitum*, waiting for the signal produced by the sensory

DOI: 10.4324/9781003491033-17

stimulation to arrive, because the sensory signal might not arrive at all. The solution might be to sample discrete time intervals of minimum value: at the end of each interval, there would be "feeling" if no corollary discharge has cancelled the signal, or mere perception of an external object if the corollary discharge has instead cancelled the "feeling".[2]

The delay, of course, does not depend on the speed of the effector (e.g. the time it takes a limb to travel the distance to touch an object), nor does it depend on the speed at which an object that might possibly provide stimulation moves. What really matters is the *variation* in stimulation (again, the difference). A fine example of such independence is provided by the way in which organisms can calculate the precise moment at which they are likely to collide with an approaching sighted object.

The origin of the idea can be found in the novel *The Black Cloud* (1957), in which astronomer and cosmologist Fred Hoyle recounts the discovery by a group of scientists at the Mount Palomar Observatory of a gigantic cloud of interstellar gas approaching Earth. In the first few chapters of the book, after the initial detection of the object, the scientists talk to each other about how to calculate the moment when the cloud will impact on our planet and wonder how the speed at which the cloud is moving can be calculated. One of them, however, observes at one point that knowing the speed of the cloud is irrelevant.

"Sorry, I don't understand all this," interjected Weichart. "I don't see why you need the speed of the cloud. You can calculate straight away how long the cloud is going to take to reach us. Here, let me do it. My guess is that the answer will turn out at much less than fifty years."

For the second time, Weichart left his seat, went to the blackboard, and cleaned off his previous drawings.

"Could we have Jensen's two slides again, please?"

When Emerson had flashed them up, first one then the other, Weichart asked: "Could you estimate how much larger the cloud is in the second slide?"

"I would say about five per cent larger. It may be a little more or a little less, but we certainly shouldn't be far off five per cent," answered Marlowe.

"Right," Weichart continued, "let's begin by defining a few symbols."

Then followed a rather lengthy calculation, at the end of which Weichart announced:

"As you see that the black cloud will be here by August 1965, or possibly sooner if some of the present estimates have to be corrected."[3]

Measuring the speed of the cloud would seem the right way to go. Knowing how far away it is and how fast it is moving, we could estimate when the cloud will impact the Earth (assuming it is moving at a constant speed). But Dr Weichart does not need to know either the distance or the speed of the cloud. All he needs are two x-rays, taken at different times, that show how much the image of the cloud has enlarged, because when an object approaches an observer (or vice versa when an observer moves towards an object) the time after which the collision will occur can be derived from the degree of change in the image that is projected onto the retina, regardless of the distance and size of the object.

Animals as diverse as human babies, fiddler crabs, chicks and rhesus macaques, when confronted with a computer monitor showing a simple disc suddenly expanding, pull back as if to avoid being hit. Even infants do the same, which shows how learning plays a very minor role here.[4]

In the optic tectum of the pigeon, neurons have been found to have a peak in discharge response just before contact with an apparently rapidly approaching stimulus occurs. And, as predicted by Weichart/Hoyle, the response of these neurons is constant over a wide range of different stimulus speeds and sizes.[5] The response to variation in stimulation is what matters.

The physicist John G. Taylor (1931–2012) tried to use the idea of delay in another way, i.e. by assuming that the corollary discharge signal is retained in a temporal memory and that its brief persistence, prior to its annihilation following the arrival of the sensory signal at the comparator, provides the sensory signal itself with the sense of "ownership" and "agency" that defines conscious experience.[6] The difficulty here, however, is that the attributes of the experience would not seem to be proper to the sensory signal itself but to the corollary discharge. In our example of the moving finger, the sense of ownership – and of being the agent (author) of the sensation – would therefore refer to the movement of the finger rather than to the sensation encountered. In the case where the finger did not move but instead encountered the object due to a displacement of the latter, there could be no sensation, as is the case. The knot unravels, however, if we assess the sensory signal for what it is, or rather what it must have been originally: a bodily reaction, i.e. a movement in its own right.

Let us try to explore this idea, not necessarily incompatible with what has been said so far, albeit somewhat heterodox. Essentially, the principle of reafference states that the organism is able to predict the sensory consequence of its own action, i.e. the stimulation that should occur as a result of its movements. However, one could also consider the situation in reverse, i.e. that the organism is able to predict the type of motor consequence, i.e. the bodily reaction, that should result from its sensory activity. In fact, this is exactly what happens, because we have so far assumed, following Reid and Humphrey, that sensation is in fact a bodily reaction, hence ultimately a motor action itself. When I touch something, for it to be possible to establish whether "I *feel* it", i.e. whether it has happened to me, it would then be sufficient for a corollary, sensory/body signal to be sent along with the sensory signal, which the comparator compares with the motor corollary signal ("delayed" of course, because the latter has happened earlier). In this case, the two corollary signals cancel each other out and therefore I have no sensation, only perception: the sensory signal escapes undisturbed and alone from the comparator: there is something out there. Conversely, if something touches me, in order to establish whether I *feel* it, the sensory/body signal is sent to the comparator: since there is no motor signal – for I did not move – it is registered that something happened on the membrane. The sensory signal that was lying in wait in the comparator is in this case loaded with the properties of a bodily action: the signal is mine, it belongs to me, I am the agent and author of it because I enacted it on the membrane as a bodily reaction. The trick is always the same, but if we look at it from the sensory/body side, we can fully explain the birth of "feeling".

Let us try again with a concrete example (see Figure 16.1). First case: I move a finger with an active movement and, by so doing, at a certain moment I encounter an object. The immediate result, if I do not focus my attention on the finger, is that there is something out there: the object of my

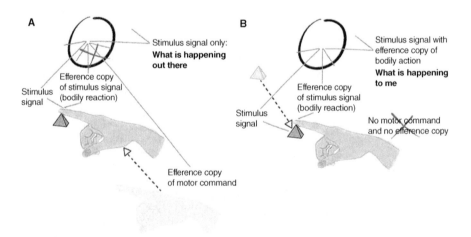

**FIGURE 16.1** (A) The movement of the hand is linked to an efference copy that annihilates the efference copy due to the local bodily reaction, thus giving rise to the perception of an object out there without sensation; (B) The object is moving and hits the finger; in the absence of any active hand movement, there is no efference copy of active motion to annihilate the efference copy associated with the local bodily reaction, thus a sensation (what is happening to me) occurs.

*Source:* Drawing courtesy of Elena Lorenzi. See for further details Vallortigara, G. (2021), "The rose and the fly. A conjecture on the origin of consciousness". *Biochemical and Biophysical Research Communications*, 564: 170–174. doi: 10.1016/j.bbrc.2020.11.005; Vallortigara, G. (2021), "The efference copy signal as a key mechanism for consciousness". *Frontiers in Systems Neuroscience*, 26, doi:10.3389/fnsys.2021.765646.

perception. What has happened is that the signal associated with the sensory/ body reaction occurring on the surface of the finger has been sent to a comparator which has annihilated it, because a corollary motor signal relating to the command for the movement of the finger has also reached the comparator. Second case: my finger stands still, there is no active movement, but some object has come upon it, stimulating its surface. The immediate result is that something has happened on the surface of my finger. The sensory/body signal produced by the stimulation was sent to the comparator, but this time it was not cancelled out by any active movement signal of the finger itself. I now feel something on my finger, something that has happened to me.

In short, what we call feeling would be nothing more than the sensory signal, retained over time, awaiting revelation (as in Borges' famous mention of an "imminence of a revelation which is never produced"[7]), i.e. a comparison between the sensory/body corollary signal and the efferent copy of a motor action that may or may not have already occurred. So yes, a memory, but of a particular kind because it is in fact a memory of a bodily reaction, which carries with it the sense of having been performed (hence the sense of belonging and authorship of the sensation) and its hedonic value: it is beneficial, I leave my finger there; it is harmful, I move it away...

In short, I am imagining that there are two complementary efferent copies: one that is the copy of the organism's command for movement; the other that is the copy of the sensory signal itself understood as bodily reaction, and therefore motor activity, a corollary discharge itself. I have no direct evidence for this hypothesis, but it seems plausible to me because the anatomy offers ample evidence of centrifugal connections within sensory systems. For example, in mammals the fibres of the visual pathway project from the retina to a nucleus in the thalamus called the lateral geniculate body, and from there to the visual cortex. However, the lateral geniculate body does not only receive this information "from below", because the main input to the geniculate actually comes "from above", from the cortex itself, and constitutes 80 per cent of the excitatory synapses. The action of these synapses is probably inhibited when a signal is generated for an active eye movement.

This is probably the right time to return to blindsight (p. 67), the phenomenon whereby certain patients with lesions to the primary visual cortex are able to show residual visual abilities, without these being accompanied by any subjective experience. The enigmatic aspect of blindsight is that patients must be *convinced* they can see in order to reveal their abilities. They seem to lack the ability to recognise visual activity as *their own* activity: the sense that "seeing" belongs to them as something they do, not as something that simply happens to them. The reason, I believe, may be the absence of the massive input back from the cortex to the geniculate, which, under normal conditions, would provide the corollary discharge of the sensory signal itself, the bodily reaction.

In short, once one admits that what appears to be a sensory signal, or a copy of it, is – or was originally – in fact a bodily reaction, i.e. a motor signal or its efferent copy (remember, the first photoreceptors were actually modified cilia), the passage of the signal to the comparison phase (in the absence of a corollary discharge associated with an active movement) leaves the hedonic value to the stimulus (I like it, I don't like it) and the specificity of the response itself. Specificity refers to the fact that the "feeling" has a precise content, a quality (at this precise moment, the "greenness" of the grass in the garden that I look at from the window, the "warmth" of the cup I hold between my fingers…). As Humphrey noted, these contents are originally derived from the type of bodily reactions to which stimuli gave rise in the different districts of our ancestors' membranes. They are therefore contingent, i.e. linked to evolutionary history, but they are not arbitrary.

Let me emphasise, once again, that whatever the right way to describe the circuit that is necessary, in its minimal configuration, for there to be "feeling", the fundamental message always remains the same: information dwells in differences. "Hearing" can only refer to some difference. As long as organisms did not move and were not faced with the problem of distinguishing between a stimulation caused by an external stimulus arriving at the surface of the organism and a stimulation caused by the active movement of the organism whose surface encountered an external stimulus, there was no difference, and therefore no sensation.[8]

## Notes

1 William James was perhaps the first to emphasise the need for neural activity of adequate duration for consciousness to emerge from the relevant input (W. James (1890), *Principles of Psychology*. Macmillan, London).

2 In the absence of stimulation, in terms of the sensation/perception pair, everything is silent, but the underlying activity of the neurons is certainly not silent. As we have noted, von Holst thought of the nervous system as characterised by an intrinsic endogenous rhythm of stimulation by certain cells, in which, however, any action on the part of the effector is blocked by – also endogenous – activity but of an inhibitory type, caused by other cells connected to the receptor. Stimulation of the receptor would cause the inhibitory activity to cease, allowing the action to take place. We could imagine a similar pattern for sensation, in which the cell (or cells) undertakes rhythmic oscillatory activity that is normally inhibited by the rhythmic inhibitory activity of other cells connected to the receptor. Cells with excitatory activity are responsible for sensation when a stimulation breaks down the inhibition. When the corollary discharge inhibits the sensation signal on the receptor side, only the signal responsible for perception remains.

3 The details of Weichart's remarks and work while at the blackboard were as follows:

"Write $\alpha$ for the present angular diameter of the cloud, measured in radians,
   d  for the linear diameter of the cloud,
   D  for its distance from Earth,
   V  for its velocity of approach,
   T  for the time required for it to reach the solar system.

To make a start, evidently we have $\alpha$ = d/D

Differentiate this equation with respect to time t, we get

$$\frac{d\alpha}{dt} = \frac{-d}{D^2}\frac{dD}{dt}$$

But $V = -\dfrac{dD}{dt}$, so therefore we can write $\dfrac{d\alpha}{dt} = \dfrac{d}{D^2}$ V.

Also we have $\dfrac{D}{V} = T$. Hence we can get rid of V, arriving at:

$$\frac{d\alpha}{dt} = \frac{d}{DT}$$

This is turning out easier than I thought. Here's the answer already: $T = \infty\,\dfrac{dt}{d\alpha}$.

The last step is to approximate $\dfrac{dt}{d\alpha}$ by finite intervals, $\dfrac{\Delta t}{\Delta\alpha}$, where $\Delta t$ = 1 month corresponding to the time difference between Dr Jensen's two plates; and from what Dr Marlowe has estimated $\Delta\alpha$ is about 5 per cent of $\alpha$, i.e. $\dfrac{\infty}{\Delta\alpha} = 20$. Therefore T = 20 $\Delta t$ = 20 months."

Taken from F. Hoyle (1957), *The Black Cloud*. Heinemann, London pp. 16–17.

4 W. Schiff (1965), "Perception of impending collision; a study of visually directed avoidant behaviour". *Psychological Monographs*, 1965, 79 Whole #604. See also M. Hebert, E. Versace and G. Vallortigara (2019), "Inexperienced preys know when to flee or to freeze in front of a threat". *Proceedings of the National Academy of Sciences USA*, 116: 22918–22920; first published 28 October 2019, doi:10.1073/pnas.1915504116.

5 Y. Wang and B. J. Frost (1992), "Time to collision is signaled by neurons in the nucleus rotundus of pigeons". *Nature*, 356: 236–238.

6 To do this, Taylor introduces a complication, namely the idea that the corollary discharge is no longer simply derived from the motor signal, but from attention. This corollary discharge from the movement of attention would be retained in a working memory by providing the properties of experience to the sensory signal before being erased by it. See J. G. Taylor (1999), *The Race for Consciousness*. MIT Press, Cambridge, Mass.; J. G. Taylor (2003), "Paying Attention to Consciousness". *Progress in Neurobiology*, 71: 30533; J. G. Taylor (2002), "Paying attention to consciousness". *Trends in Cognitive Sciences*, 5: 206–210.

7 J. L. Borges ([1944]1962), *Ficciones* [Fictions]. Grove Press, New York.

8 What about plants? In principle, it would not be impossible to conceive of an efferent copying mechanism in plants, but the problem is that in the absence of active movement there is no way to signal that displacement has occurred or the command for displacement. It could be argued that displacement as such is sufficient to perform the same function, but signalling that a source of stimulation is the product of a displacement of the plant whose surface has encountered the stimulus itself, rather than the stimulus impacting the plant's surface, would require very long memories. When the stimulation arrives at the surface and a copy is sent to the comparator, the comparison should be made for a displacement that may have started a few weeks or a few hundred years earlier. In the case of relatively fast reactions such as those of, for example, the mimosa pudica (*Mimosa pudica* L.) the response is always consequent and therefore subsequent to the stimulus, and invariably connected to the stimulus, so that any feedforward mechanism by the

response itself on the sensory signal is precluded. I happened to attend some remarkable presentations by the plant neurobiologist Stefano Mancuso, over the course of which some seedlings (of beans, if I remember correctly) moved until they encountered potential supports, but I cannot say whether there is any evidence of a feedback circuit that cancels out a sensation of contact as a result of the displacement, nor whether this displacement can be qualified as active movement rather than growth. See S. Mancuso and A. Viola (2015), *Verde brillante* [Brilliant green]. Giunti, Florence; and for the whole diatribe on so-called "plant neurobiology", see E. Brenner, R. Stahlberg, S. Mancuso, J. Vivanco, F. Baluška and E. Van Volkenburgh (2006), "Plant neurobiology: An integrated view of plant signaling", *Trends in Plant Sciences*, 11: 413–419; A. Alpi et al. (2007), "Plant neurobiology: No brain, no gain?". *Trends in Plant Sciences*, 12, 135–136; L. Taiz, D. Alkon, A. Draguhn, A. Murphy, M. Blatt, C. Hawes, G. Thiel and D. G. Robinson (2019), "Plants neither possess nor require consciousness". *Trends in Plant Sciences*, 3 July 2019, online: doi:10.1016/j.tplants.2019.05.008; ten Cate, C. (2023), "Plant sentience: A hypothesis based on shaky premises". *Animal Sentience*, 33(13); J. Mallatt, D. G. Robinson, M. R. Blatt, A. Draguhn and L. Taiz (2023), "Plant sentience: The burden of proof". *Animal Sentience*, 33(15).

# 17

# EXPERIENCE, IN BRIEF

Even at the risk of sounding a little repetitive, I think it may be worthwhile briefly summarising the natural history of experience as I have told it to you so far, in order to recognise the crucial aspects, both in the similarities and differences with the thinking of other authors. As I noted previously, the fabric has largely been woven by others, while I have merely sought to tie up a number of old threads. So let us see if the weave holds.

Thomas Reid first suggested distinguishing what happens to us (sensation) from what happens out there (perception). And we have learned from neurological studies how perception can in fact be unconscious, for example in blindsight. Nicholas Humphrey, echoing and developing Reid's arguments, also pointed out how sensation appears to retain the characteristics of a bodily response, as it probably occurred originally in early organisms. In this book, I have asked when and for what reason the need to distinguish sensation and perception appeared.

The first organisms endowed with active movement found themselves called upon to produce a splitting in an otherwise unitary sensory signal: does something touch you because it came towards you or because you, by moving, moved towards it? The artifice that can allow this splitting is the phenomenon of efferent copying or corollary discharge, which we have known about in detail since the early years of the last century, thanks to the work of Erich von Holst and Roger Sperry (but which had already been intuited by many other scholars well before them). Every time the organism performs an active movement, a copy of the movement command is generated and compared with the incoming sensory signal, so that the latter is cancelled out. As many authors have noted, this efferent copy mechanism actually constitutes a primitive distinction between self and non-self: a crucial step in the

DOI: 10.4324/9781003491033-18

emergence of consciousness (i.e. experience, in the sense of the term we use here). But how can the efferent copy mechanism *produce* experience?

Experience, if we follow Reid and Humphrey's intuitions, is associated with sensation, with what happens to us, and would therefore manifest itself precisely when the efferent copy signal is not present, i.e. when the sensory signal is not annihilated by the corollary discharge. Note, in this regard, that almost all authors seem to believe the opposite, because by not distinguishing between sensation and perception, they associate the role of motor action with perception (p. 86).

The corollary discharge signal was not present originally, when organisms without active movement reacted to stimuli with a mere bodily contraction (stimulus arrives on the membrane, the membrane wrinkles…). What gives the sensory signal of actively moving organisms the possibility (although we ought to say the necessity) of experience? My proposal is that if we accept that the original sensory response was a localised contraction of the body (or rather, of the membrane), an efferent copy of *this* body movement signal might have evolved in addition to the usual efferent copy resulting from active movement. And it would be the copy of the body signal that is compared in the comparator with the copy of the signal consequent to active movement. When we move an arm to meet the table with a finger, a contraction of the epidermis is produced on the surface of the finger which is very much akin to that manifested in the very earliest organisms – it matters little that now, instead of really being there on the epidermis, the contraction has been internalised in the activity of the neurons in a portion of the cortex, because in a certain sense it has remained what it was: an action or, better, a bodily re-action. Together with the sensory signal, therefore, a corollary discharge is generated that follows a reactive bodily activity: a signal that – with a bit of a delay compared with the sensory signal – then reaches the comparator. Since we have actively moved our arm, the body signal is cancelled out by this corollary motor signal. The result is that a sensory signal comes out of the comparator, which is emptied of the juice of the body reaction. Lacking the action component, that feeling is not a true feeling, an experience, because it lacks the justification provided by *ownership*, which is usually derived from the fact that the organism is the performer, i.e. the author of the bodily contraction. It is not a sensation but rather the perception of an object out there. Conversely, if the limb is not actively moved but the finger is passively stimulated, the response of the local bodily contraction cannot be cancelled out by the corollary discharge resulting from the movement of the arm; therefore, when it comes out of the comparator, the sensory signal is loaded with the bodily reaction: it has become sensation, i.e. the experience of something that has happened to the organism.

Using touch as an example is very convenient for me, because it facilitates argumentation. But the hypothesis must hold regardless of the sensory medium.[1] If vision is palpation with the gaze (see p. 33), we should be in a perpetual state of perception without sensation, for our eyes move incessantly. This may indeed be the case, because associated with saccadic movements, which are active movements, there is so-called "saccadic suppression". To realise this, just try staring alternately at your right eye and your left eye in front of a mirror; your eyes will appear to be motionless because during the saccade (the movement by which you move your gaze from one eye to the other), your vision is suppressed. If you try to do the same in front of a camera that introduces a short delay between your eye movement and the return of the image, you will see your eyes move (the same happens when observing a friend who shifts their gaze from one eye to the other in front of a mirror, because in this case you are not the one producing the eye movement).[2]

## Notes

1 With the neuroscientist Gian Domenico Iannetti, who is a great expert on the cerebral bases of pain, I briefly discussed the possibility that a purely proximal response such as pain only appeared after the advent of feedforward mechanisms such as corollary discharge, because in my opinion before that there must have been only nociception, i.e. no experience of pain. Different from tickling, if we actively touch something that is hot, we have pain. I wonder however whether it has the same phenomenal quality of when something hot touches us. More bravely, I wonder whether only in the second case we really *feel* pain and in the first we rather react to nociception. The question certainly deserves further study, for which, however, I do not yet feel sufficiently prepared. In the meantime, see the important work by Gian Domenico Iannetti (A. Moureaux and G. D. Iannetti (2018), "The search for pain biomarkers in the human brain". *Brain*, 141: 3290–3307; F. Mancini, C. F. Sambo, J. D. Ramirez, D. L. K. Bennett, P. Haggard and G. D. Iannetti (2013), "A fovea for pain at the fingertips". *Current Biology*, 23: 495: 500).
2 The matter is probably different for ocular tremors, which cause the contours of the observed object to fade due to receptor fatigue; however, in this case, even if the object fades, the sensation referring to the rest of the visual field (the background) does not disappear.

# 18

# HEARING THE SONG OF THE CRICKET THAT IS NOT THERE

Playing with cells
the game of corpses:
the toads and dragonflies
the roses and the poppies.

Guido Gozzano

It is precisely the need for a comparison of signals that makes the presence of another neuron necessary, in addition to the sensory and motor neurons, an interneuron (as in *D*, Figure 14.2. The interneuron does not communicate with the outside world, neither towards a receptor (as the sensory neuron does) nor towards a muscle (as the motor neuron does), but is connected only with other neurons (as in Figure 14.2, with the sensory and motor neurons).

In the nervous system of the cricket (*Gryllus bimaculatus*), for example, a single interneuron spans the entire nervous system of the animal, with rich arborisations in each ganglion. This interneuron appears to be in charge of mediating the efferent copy (i.e. corollary discharge) of the cricket's song.[1]

There is an old story that is told to students about the dangers of drawing hasty conclusions from experiments. It goes like this. A scientist wants to understand how the cricket perceives sounds. He places the cricket on the table, makes a loud clapping sound and observes that the cricket jumps out of fright. He picks up the cricket, removes one of its legs and repeats the operation: when the sound is presented, again the cricket jumps. Then the scientist proceeds to remove a second leg, but again the cricket jerks when the sound is produced. The scientist then proceeds to amputate the other legs, one by one, always with the same result. He finally arrives at the amputation of the sixth and last leg. He lays the cricket on the table and it no longer moves when the sound is presented. The

DOI: 10.4324/9781003491033-19

scientist may thus conclude: "As you may observe, the cricket hears sounds with its legs!" Irony would have it that he is right, albeit for the wrong reasons. The cricket, like many insects, actually has hearing organs on its front limbs (tarsi).

The cricket's song is generated by rubbing the elytra (the front wings). However, the hearing sensors located on the tarsi are active while the animal produces its song. How can it distinguish its own sounds from those of another animal or avoid the habituation of continuously hearing sounds that it produces itself? The answer is that the animal's auditory pathways are inhibited by a corollary discharge (an efferent copy) in sync with the production of sounds. If the activity of the auditory neurons in the proto-thoracic ganglion is recorded simultaneously with that of the interneuron, we may observe that the activity of the latter occurs in coincidence with the activity of the motor neurons that innervate the wing muscles and with the inhibition of the activity of the auditory sensory neurons on its front legs. When the wing is used for the function of flight, thus without producing sound, interneuron activity is inhibited.

What could be the consequence for the cricket of a malfunction of the interneuron of the corollary discharge? The interneuron, which sends the efferent copy to the centres that analyse the stimulation, signals in carbon copy that the activity is not external but self-generated. If the corollary discharge mechanism did not work, the effect for the cricket would mean it would no longer recognise the sound it produces as its own. The cricket would experience a hallucination: it would hear the voice of a cricket that is not there...

Hearing voices, as is well known, is one of the most clinically relevant symptoms for the diagnosis of schizophrenia; auditory hallucinations have an average prevalence of 60 per cent in individuals with schizophrenic disorders.

We all continuously engage in so-called inner dialogue, without the need to speak out loud. The Russian psychologist Lev Vygotsky (1896–1934) hypothesised that inner dialogue develops through a process of internalisation of the external dialogue, the one we hold out loud with others.[2] Indeed, the inner dialogue is also accompanied by muscular movements of the larynx, but these are minimal and can only be detected using the technique of electromyography.

It was noted that the area of the left inferior frontal gyrus (Broca's area), which is active when we speak loudly, is also activated during internal dialogue. The motor planning necessary for the production of speech that occurs at the level of this area is therefore associated with the sending of an efferent copy to the auditory cortex. When we speak, therefore, or even when we only plan to speak, limiting ourselves to internal speech, just as when the cricket sings, the auditory reafference is cancelled by the efferent copy. In schizophrenic patients, however, the failure to send the efferent copy could lead to increased activation of the auditory cortex, which would mistake the patient's own language, or motor programming, *for the voice of others.*

A disturbance in the mechanisms of efferent copying may explain other psychotic symptoms besides hearing voices, such as the impression of being under the control of external forces, which would result from the inability to predict the sensory consequences of one's actions.

Psychiatrist Irwin Feinberg was the first to hypothesise that the reafference principle might be crucial in the impairment between self and non-self that characterises schizophrenia.[3] In fact, Feinberg went much further with his hypothesis. Following the idea of the neurologist John Hughlings Jackson (1835–1911) that thought is simply the most complex expression of our motor activity, he imagined that corollary discharges, or efferent copies, may be associated with thought itself, just as they are with sensorimotor activities. In this way, the more obscure symptoms of schizophrenia would appear in an entirely new light.

Consider the case where your arm moves, but that you, in the absence of an efferent copy, are unable to tell whether you moved it yourself or whether an external cause moved it. You can simulate such a condition with a little game that many children learn at school, in the happy hours of recreation.

This is the so-called Kohnstamm effect, named after the neurologist Oskar Kohnstamm (1871–1917), who first described it.[4] Figure 18.1 shows the first documented image of the phenomenon, in which a patient is seen pushing his

**FIGURE 18.1**   The first photographic documentation of the Kohnstamm effect. The patient pushes his arms outwards while the neurologist, Dr Alberto Salmon, holds them back. Subsequently, under relaxed conditions, the patient's arms are raised involuntarily, due to a posthumous effect of contraction of the lateral deltoid muscles.

*Source:* Salmon, A. (1916), "D'un interessant phenomene d'automatisme qu'on remarque apres les efforts musculaires chez les sujets sains" [An interesting phenomenon of automatism that we notice after muscular efforts in healthy subjects]. *Revue Neurologique* (Paris), 29: 27–34.

arms outwards with as much force as possible, while the doctor, the neurologist Salmon, holds them back. After a minute or so, the patient is allowed to lower his arms and relax. At this point he can observe with amazement that his arms start to rise autonomously, as if pushed by an external force. If you don't have a neurologist to hold your arms still, don't worry, it works just as well with a door frame. Position yourself in the doorway, and push the backs of your hands as hard as you can for about a minute against the sides of the frame. Then take a step forward, relax your arms by letting them fall downwards and, after a moment, you will feel and see your arms magically rise to almost a horizontal position.

The precise reasons why this phenomenon occurs have not been fully elucidated,[5] but as far as the aspect that interests us here is concerned, the sensation that the arms are moved by someone else, that there is something or someone under the arms pushing them upwards, we can easily recognise its origin: the omission of the efferent copy signal. This is in fact completely missing because no message has been sent from the motor programming areas to move the arms upwards.

As argued by Feinberg, the distortions of one's body boundaries so often reported by schizophrenic patients could be interpreted as disturbances in the corollary discharge/efference copy mechanisms. If, when I move and touch something, my movement is not accompanied by an efferent copy, it follows that the boundaries of my body and those of the objects are labile and elastic. Furthermore, even when I touch my own body, the resulting stimulation will no longer be caused by me, but by someone else.

## Notes

1  J. F. A. Poulet and B. Hedwig (2006), "The cellular basis of a corollary discharge". *Science*, 311: 518–522.
2  L. S. Vygotsky (1962), *Thought and Language*. Cambridge, MA, MIT Press.
3  I. Feinberg (1978), "Efference copy and corollary discharge: Implications for thinking and its disorders". *Schizophrenia Bulletin*, 4: 636–640. See also, for a popular exposition of the connection between corollary discharge/efferent copy and schizophrenia, A. Ananthaswamy (2015), *The Man Who Wasn't There*. Dutton, New York.
4  J. De Havas, H. Gomi and P. Haggard (2017), "Experimental investigations of control principles of involuntary movement: A comprehensive review of the Kohnstamm phenomenon". *Experimental Brain Research*, 235: 1953–1997.
5  As a result of the adaptation that occurs in the pushing phase, an input seems to be sent through the motor pathway that controls voluntary movement, producing the bizarre impression of a movement that does not belong to us.

# 19

## TICKLING YOURSELF

Tickling should be done on the brain, not in the armpits.

Renato Rascel

The itching sensation aroused by a light touch on the skin, known as "knismesis", generating an urge to rub and scratch, can serve to get rid of small insects and parasites. But the much more mysterious sensation that leads us to laugh, known as "gargalesis", i.e. heavy tickling, can usually only be provoked by another person.

Gargalesis is probably not limited to primates; when tickled, laboratory rats emit the same high-pitched squeak as when playing with each other.[1] In our species, the body parts most sensitive to tickling are also those most vulnerable in hand-to-hand combat, which has suggested that tickling might confer an advantage by prompting individuals to protect these sensitive parts more carefully. This does not, however, explain why tickling should stimulate laughter. An idea formulated by psychologist Robert Provine[2] is that tickling has evolved as a means of communication between parents and their children: laughter in response to touch may be a positive feedback for parents, which would thus encourage them to carry on, allowing the game to continue and thus ensuring its formative value for the little ones.

The fact that it can only be elicited by another individual might lead one to believe that tickling is a form of explicit communication. In actual fact, tickle sensitivity is an automatic physiological reaction, a behaviour over which we have no conscious control. The reason we cannot tickle ourselves does not depend on a psychological recognition of the other person's role, but is related to the mechanism of efferent copying.

When you move your hand trying to tickle yourself under the armpit, an efferent copy of your motor activity is sent to the sensory system, cancelling

DOI: 10.4324/9781003491033-20

out the sensory signal itself. Neuroscientist Sarah-Jayne Blakemore has measured brain activity while people are tickled by another person or attempt to
tickle themselves. In the first case, the somatosensory cortex (the part of the
brain responsible for touch) and the anterior cingulate cortex (which handles the sense of gratification and impulse control) are activated. In the second case, these areas remain relatively inactive, while the cerebellum (which
handles the coordination and regulation of muscular activity) is activated. It
therefore appears that the cerebellum is involved in the prediction of specific
sensations induced by certain movements, reducing the reaction of the somatosensory and anterior cingulate cortices.

The adaptive value of a mechanism that prevents self-arousal is obvious:
it would not be a good thing to go around giggling every time you reach into
your pocket for a handkerchief and happen to touch yourself. However, one
might wonder why in knismesis, which is elicited by very weak tactile stimuli,
no efferent copying mechanism seems to operate, given that in this case we
feel the itch even when we ourselves provide the stimulation. I believe that
in fact the efferent copying mechanism is at work here as well. Try moving
your finger by lightly touching the skin on the back of your hand. You will
not start laughing as in the case of the gargalesis, but you will certainly feel
a tactile sensation, an itch. Note, however, that your membrane has been
stimulated in two areas, for each of which you might expect an itching sensation: the back of the hand and the surface of the finger itself. However, the
sensation is limited to the back of your hand; there is no localised sensation
on the finger. This is because the active part of the motor action is related to
the finger itself, and it is therefore the sensory signal on the epidermis of the
finger that is cancelled by the corollary discharge (efference copy).

What happens, then, with the tickle proper, i.e. gargalesis? The tactile sensations are not cancelled out by the corollary discharge. When you try to
tickle your armpits, you do not laugh, but you undoubtedly feel a sensation.
In fact, what people report is that there is a gradation of sensations, from
feeling something tactilely to the explicit sensation of being tickled, which appears to be, by the way, highly variable from individual to individual (some
people react paroxysmally to the mere threat of being tickled, in the absence
of any stimulation). But this is exactly what Sarah-Jayne Blakemore and colleagues observed: a *reduction in* activity in the somatosensory areas and the
anterior cingulate cortex, not its complete cancellation. The gradation in the
modulation of cortical activity probably depends on both the intensity of
tactile stimulation (which above a certain threshold activates the cingulate
cortex) and the intensity of the efferent copy signal.

It seems clear that, although dependent on activity in the somatosensory
cortex, tickling is not reducible to tactile stimulation: as we note, laughter and
defensive manoeuvres are often observed without (or prior to) the person being
tactilely stimulated. Experiments with rats confirm these observations. When

tickled on the belly by an experimenter's hand, rats emit characteristic 50 kHz ultrasonic vocalisations that are associated with a positive valence. The experience of being tickled appears to be rewarding for the animals, which actively seek it out, spontaneously approaching the hand to look for the tickle again and accompanying this with characteristic little jumps like those observed in play behaviour. If, while the animal is being tickled, we record the activity of its neurons in the region of the somatosensory cortex, where that part of the belly that is being stimulated is represented, we may observe intense activity in many neurons (while others become completely silent). The interesting thing is that some of these neurons increase their activity just as the rats approach the tickling hand, i.e. before stimulation has taken place.

It appears that some schizophrenic patients are capable of tickling themselves, particularly those in whom one observes symptoms such as auditory hallucinations or the feeling that one's actions and thoughts are controlled from the outside. These patients probably represent the pathological extreme of a continuum in the efficiency of efferent copy feedforward mechanisms. Indeed, even psychologically healthy individuals who have high scores on scales measuring schizophrenic-like personality traits, individuals endowed with a vivid imagination, for example, and those prone to mild forms of paranoid behaviour, can to varying degrees tickle themselves.[3]

Even for people who do not show any schizophrenic traits, there is a way to tickle themselves. The trick is to introduce a slight time delay between the completion of the motor action and the subsequent sensory stimulation. Sarah-Jayne Blakemore used an apparatus for this purpose in which people could move a mechanical arm back and forth with one hand; the movement was transferred to a second robotic arm that had a piece of foam rubber attached to the end with which the palm of the other hand was stimulated. When people are stimulated in this way, indirectly but still controlled by the movement of their own hand, they do not feel any particular tickle. However, if the robot transfers the stimulation to the palm with a delay of just 100 to 300 milliseconds, an intense tickle is felt. The short time delay is sufficient to fool the predictive properties of the feedforward system of efferent copying about the consequences of the subject's action, bringing the situation back to that of an external rather than self-generated stimulation.

### Notes

1 J. Panksepp and J. Burgdorf (1999), "Laughing rats? Playful tickling arouses high-frequency ultrasonic chirping in young rodents". In *Toward a Science of Consciousness III*, S. R. Hameroff, D. Chalmers and A. W. Kaszniak (eds.), pp. 231–244, MIT Press, New York.
2 R. R. Provine (2000), *Laughter. A Scientific Investigation*. Faber, London.
3 A. Lemaitre, M. Luyat and G. Lafargue (2016), "Individuals with pronounced schizotypal traits are particularly successful in tickling themselves". *Consciousness and Cognition*, 41: 64–71.

# 20

# THE COROLLARY DISCHARGE OF THOUGHT

In a rather resentful note published in *Psychiatric Times* in 2010, Feinberg lamented how the idea that the positive symptoms of schizophrenia, such as auditory hallucinations, are due to a defect in the efferent copying system is often ascribed to cognitive neuroscientist Christopher Frith, when in fact he had spoken about it almost 15 years earlier.[1] As can be seen, history repeats itself: ideas linking the principle of reafference to various aspects of consciousness have been circulating for many years, in the writings of numerous authors.

However, there is no doubt in specific terms: Feinberg not only first came up with the idea that a defect in the efferent copy underlies schizophrenic disorders, but extended it to ordinary thought processes, thus prompting a crucial question even outside the realm of psychopathology, a question that concerns us all: how do we know our thoughts are "ours"? You will notice the similarity with the problem already mentioned for blindsight: How do I know that what I see is me seeing it? That the perception belongs to me? In the case of thought, the question is even more intriguing. Thoughts often seem to come to us in an erratic, whimsical and unpredictable way. We say, "I don't know why this thought came to me." But in normal conditions, in the absence of pathology, we have no doubt that that thought, of unknown origins, is nevertheless *our* thought.

Let us try to apply the line of reasoning employed so far for sense-motor mechanisms to thoughts. Could it be that, in the absence of corollary discharge, of efferent copying of mental processes, our own thoughts no longer belong to us but are instead, like the voices heard by schizophrenics, the thoughts of *others*?

When Wilder Penfield (1891–1976), the famous Canadian neurosurgeon, stimulated areas of the motor cortex with an electrode during the exploratory

DOI: 10.4324/9781003491033-21

phase of an operation to treat epilepsy, in some instances patients found themselves moving an arm as a result of the brain stimulation. They claimed, however, that it was not they who had moved the limb, but that the surgeon had moved it. In the absence of an autonomous movement or the intention to make it, no corollary discharge or efferent copy is generated; the patients cannot attribute the cause of the arm movement to themselves, so they attribute it to some external agent.

Likewise, when patients are afflicted by a thought or belief that, despite the lack of evidence, they cannot help but accept, this could reflect the absence of an appropriate corollary discharge associated with their own mental activity. The experience so typical of schizophrenic disorder of being controlled by other people or supernatural agents could be the patients' way of trying to account for the fact that certain thoughts seem to arise independently, i.e. unrelated to their usual generator – the subject him- or herself.

What Feinberg proposes is that efferent copying mechanisms operate at the highest levels of the integrative functions of the nervous system, at the level of thought, which would be a sophisticated form of motor act, distinguishing between those thought activities that are self-generated by the subject and those externally induced.[2]

That a corollary discharge mechanism is present in thought can be deduced from the findings of Penfield's own experiments. Not only do patients attribute the origin of limb movement to the surgeon rather than themselves, but also the memories they recall as a result of the stimulation are not recognised as their own. When the Penfield electrode stimulated the temporal lobe, patients experienced memories, but they described them by telling the surgeon "You made me think of this." The patient is no longer the author of his or her own thoughts, for no efferent copy of these thoughts is produced; they are therefore thoughts generated by others.

### Notes

1 C. D. Frith (1992), *The Cognitive Neuropsychology of Schizophrenia*. Hove, UK: Lawrence Erlbaum Associates; Feinberg I. (1978), "Efference copy and corollary discharge: Implications for thinking and its disorders". *Schizophrenia Bulletin*, 4: 636–640.

2 I. Feinberg and M. Guazzelli (1999), "Schizophrenia – a disorder of the corollary discharge systems that integrate the motor systems of thought with the sensory systems of consciousness". *British Journal of Psychiatry*, 174: 196–204; I. Feinberg (2011), "Corollary discharge, hallucinations, and dreaming". *Schizophrenia Bulletin*, 37: 1–3.

# 21

# FEELING AND COGITATING

Perhaps you did not believe me to be a man of logic.

Dante Alighieri

Many scholars in the field of cognitive neuroscience and philosophy of mind believe the potential for feeling can be diagnosed from the complexity of the nervous system. In light of what we have said so far, this hypothesis seems incongruous. There are systems made up of numerous neurons, such as the cerebellum, that have nothing to do (at least directly[1]) with consciousness. The psychiatrist and neuroscientist Giulio Tononi tried to get around this problem by arguing that the substratum of consciousness must reside in a system composed of many functionally different elements that are, however, closely interconnected to form a highly integrated whole. While I admire his work, it seems to me that what Tononi calls "integrated information" is, precisely, a measure of information: something that does not provide a necessary (let alone sufficient) reason for consciousness, understood as sentience, sensation.[2] I feel the same dissatisfaction with other famous models of consciousness, such as Bernard Baars' and Stanislas Dehaene's "Global Workspace".[3] They seem to me models of "cogitating", not of "feeling". Indeed, I can imagine that the complexity of the nervous system could be linked – with a degree of specification – to computing power, and thus to the speed of information processing or memory. But what kind of link should there be between complexity and consciousness? What property of complexity would *explain* the property of having experiences?

I also find erroneous the corollary of the hypothesis, namely that the presence of consciousness can be deduced from the cognitive complexity manifested in behaviour, which constitutes the main argument of so much

DOI: 10.4324/9781003491033-22

animalist rhetoric: "the dog (or chimpanzee or dolphin or any other creature…) that solves a complex problem, showing, for example, glimmers of a
theory of mind: how could it thus not be sentient?" My favourite example to
refute the set of these arguments is the following.

If I tell you that Alan's brain is bigger than Bart's, and that Bart's brain
is bigger than Charles', you easily deduce that Alan's brain must be bigger
than Charles'. The problem can be made more complicated by using a larger
number of elements, e.g. with five individuals, A (Alan), B (Bart), C (Charles),
D (Donald) and E (Edward), and then asking whether B's or D's brain is
bigger. Pigeons, chickens, monkeys and fish are all capable of solving transitive inference problems.[4] Possessing such capabilities seems to make the
hypothesis that we are dealing with sentient beings persuasive. How is it possible to be able to draw a transitive inference without being sentient?

An interesting fact, moreover, is that bees apparently cannot solve transitive
inference problems, which are instead feasible for monkeys, chickens, fish,
pigeons, mice and humans.[5] A difference that, at least in part, might reha-
bilitate the Aristotelian idea of *Scala Naturae*. However, as Sherlock Holmes
noted, when a fact seems to disprove a long chain of deductions, it is invariably
open to an alternative interpretation. Let me try to offer you such an interpretation, based on two arguments. First, bees cannot solve transitive inference
problems not because their reasoning abilities are limited but because of the
way their memory is organised. Second, fish, chickens, pigeons, monkeys and
humans with their large, memory-intensive brains can solve transitive inference problems, but *independently of the* fact that they are conscious.

Let us see the method by which transitive inference problems are proposed
to organisms that do not possess language (Figure 21.1). First, they are made

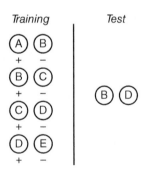

*Training*      Test

**FIGURE 21.1** In the transitive inference test, the animal first learns a series of
premises, e.g. that in the pair A–B the rewarded stimulus is A and
the unrewarded stimulus is B; that in the pair B–C the rewarded
stimulus is B and the unrewarded stimulus is C, and so on. At the
time of the test, the animal must choose between B and D, which
have never been presented together.

to learn the premises of the problem. Instead of names, we can use any visual stimuli for elements A, B, C, D and E. For example, the pigeons learn that in the pair A–B, stimulus A is associated with a reward (birdseed); in the pair B–C, stimulus B is associated with a reward; in the pair C–D, stimulus C is associated with a reward, and so on… Once these pairs (the problem premises) are well acquired, the animals are presented with a new pair, never seen before, even though its two elements, B and D, are well known. The correct answer is that B will be associated with the reward. Note that during the training phase, the two stimuli B and D were either rewarded or unrewarded exactly the same number of times (e.g. B is unrewarded in pair A–B but rewarded in pair B–C, while D is unrewarded in pair C–D and rewarded in pair D–E). It would thus seem that there is no way to derive a greater associative strength for B than for D and, in general, to derive a hierarchical order of the type A>B>C>D>E.

Actually, there is a way, if one reflects not on the reward assignments, but on the *absence* of these assignments. Consider the pair A–B, where A is rewarded and B is unrewarded. Obviously, A is *always* rewarded and tends to be more and more chosen during the various trials. Consequently, B will certainly be less chosen, but for this reason also less penalised, and this will favour it in the pairing B–C. In contrast, consider now the pair D–E, where D is rewarded and E is always unrewarded. Obviously, E is always unrewarded and this favours the choice of D. But the choice of D implies the choice for the unrewarded stimulus in the pair C–D. In short, since the extremes A and E are always rewarded and unrewarded respectively, the stimuli that are more contiguous to them will gain (B) or lose (D) some attractiveness, while C will be found to have an intermediate value in the ranking. In fact, A>B>C>D>E…

If you have a headache at this point, take comfort in the fact that many people find it difficult to solve the five-stimulus version of the problem when it is presented to them in the direct form of an intelligence test. What happens, however, if we try to make a fair interspecies comparison between solvers of different species? For example, a comparison between humans and pigeons, in which a series of trials are proposed during which the premises of the problem are learnt.

Before proceeding with the tournament, however, let us return for a moment to the bottom of the class, those who do not make it: the bees. Now that we know what kind of simple calculations might underlie the correct choice (B, in the pair B versus D), we can see where the bees' difficulty lies, if difficulty it is. A detailed analysis of the bees' choices during the tests showed that they form an associative hierarchy, e.g. they choose A over D. So, if they are influenced by the reward/non-reward ratio, why does this effect not also extend to the pairs adjacent to A and E, such as the pairs B–C and C–D? The problem, it seems, is that bees' memory is characterised by a very strong "recency" effect, i.e. a particularly vivid memory of the last pair in the sequence, the pair D–E, in which D is rewarded. In a nutshell, while the reward/non-reward ratio would cause the bees to choose B in the B–D pair, the strong recency of D would compensate for the greater associative strength of B, causing them to choose at random. The reason why the last choice is so remarkable is probably due to the fact that in a natural environment it is convenient for bees to persistently take nectar from the same type of flowers, without changing as long as these continue to offer a profitable reward.[6]

Now we come to the comparison that interests us, the one between organisms that instead solve the task. The German scientist Juan Delius reproduced the experiment with a group of university students just as it is usually conducted with pigeons.[7] Without any verbal instructions, the students simply participate in a game in which they are shown two doors each marked with a stimulus and, each time, it is a matter of working out which of the two doors leads to a prize (university credits instead of birdseed…). There are five stimuli in total, A, B, C, D and E, the same as those used for pigeons. When learning is achieved, the B–D pair is presented every so often, interspersed with the other pairs. What happens? Well, Delius made an extraordinary discovery. The students who solve the problem, that is, who give the right answer, fall into two categories, roughly of the same number. There are the "explicit" solvers, who can say what the nature of the problem is and how they solved it, and then there are the "implicit" solvers, who claim that, when faced with the pairs B–D, they simply guessed… These subjects, who guessed, however, show the same success rate and the same number of errors as the explicit solvers. They solve the inference problem without being aware of it, without being conscious of the problem and the solution. In the cognitive domain, they resemble patients who show the phenomenon of blindsight in the perceptual domain.

Patients with blindsight exhibit adequate visual behaviour while denying having any experience of seeing. Likewise, Delius' students cope adequately with cognitive inference tasks without having any experience, any awareness, of either the solution they came to or the fact there was ever a problem to solve.

Studies revealing the ability of non-human animals to solve transitive inference problems, interesting and important though they may be, do not tell us that, because they are capable of complex cognitive performance, non-human animals are therefore sentient: indeed, humans conduct the same activities in the absence of consciousness. This is why theories about consciousness that postulate its appearance from some unspecified threshold of complexity of the nervous system leave me rather unimpressed. In another context, I also pointed out that it is not cognitive or intellectualistic criteria that guide us in ascribing experience to our fellow human beings. Human beings with severe cognitive handicaps may find themselves incapable of solving problems that are within the reach of a pigeon, and yet, rightly or wrongly, we consider them sentient.[8]

Borges tells us that in a fragment by the poet Coleridge, the following passage may be read: "What if you slept, and what if in your sleep you dreamed, and what if in your dream you went to heaven and there you plucked a strange and beautiful flower, and what if when you awoke you had the flower in your hand? Ah, what then?"[9]

The imagined event seems so implausible that it is probably not worth bothering to find an answer, but there might be genuine phenomena that, unexpectedly, confront us with the same kind of question. If, on studying trout, we were to discover that they possess highly complex cognitive processes, then what? Then nothing. It would not be proof that trout have access to the heaven of consciousness (or even that they dream). We have to look elsewhere for such evidence.

## Notes

1 I emphasise "directly" because the role of the cerebellum in efferent copying mechanisms highlights its indirect importance, as we have noted in the case of self-produced tickling.

2 G. Tononi (2012), *Phi: A Voyage from the Brain to the Soul*. Random House, New York; *Sizing Up Consciousness: Towards an Objective Measure of the Capacity for Experience*. Oxford University Press, Oxford; G. Tononi and M. Massimini (2017), *Nulla di più grande*. Baldini e Castoldi, Milan.

3 These models hypothesise that for incoming information to become conscious it must be represented by networks of sensory neurons, such as those in the primary visual cortex, that this representation lasts long enough to have access to a second stage of distributed processing in the cerebral cortex, and that from this combination of "bottom-up" information propagation and "top-down" information amplification, coherent activity between different brain centres is triggered through attention. This coherent activity would be what we experience as consciousness (see B. J. Baars (1988), *A Cognitive Theory of Consciousness*. Cambridge, MA: Cambridge University Press; S. Dehaene, C. Sergent and J.-P. Changeux (2003), "A neuronal network model linking subjective reports and objective physiological data during conscious perception". *Proceedings of the National Academy of Science USA*, 14: 8520–8525; S. Dehaene (2014), *Le Code de la conscience*. Paris: Odile Jacob, Paris. However, I do not see how all this can explain the emergence of experiences, not to mention the problem, discussed by neuroscientist Bjorn Merkel, concerning the evidence of consciousness in the absence of cortex, for example in children born without a cortex (B. Merkel (2007), "Consciousness without a cerebral cortex: A challenge for neuroscience and medicine". *Behavioral and Brain Sciences*, 30: 63–134).

4 The test was originally invented for pre-school children, see P. E. Bryant and T. Trabasso (1971), "Transitive inferences and memory in young children". *Nature*, 232: 456–458) and then extended to a variety of species, see for example: L. von Fersen, C. D. Wynne and J. D. Delius (1991), "Transitive inference formation in pigeons". *Journal of Experimental Psychology*, 17: 334–341; L. Grosenick, T. S. Clement and R. D. Fernald (2007), "Fish can infer social rank by observation alone". *Nature*, 445: 429–432; A. B. Bond, A. C. Kamil and R. P. Balda (2003), "Social complexity and transitive inference in corvids". *Animal Behaviour*, 65: 479–487; C. G. Paz-y-Miño, A. B. Bond, A. C. Kamil and R. P. Balda (2004), "Pinyon jays use transitive inference to predict social dominance". *Nature*, 430: 778–781; H. Daves (1992), "Transitive inference in rats (*Rattus norvegicus*)". *Journal of Comparative Psychology*, 106: 342–349; B. M. Weiß, S. Kehmeier and C. Schloegl (2010), "Transitive inference in free-living greylag geese, *Anser answer*". *Animal Behaviour*, 79: 1277–1283; E. L. MacLean, D. J. Merritt and

E. M. Brannon (2008), "Social complexity predicts transitive reasoning in prosimian primates". *Animal Behaviour*, 76: 177–182; J. N. Daisley, G. Vallortigara and L. Regolin (2010), "Logic in an asymmetrical (social) brain: Transitive inference in the young domestic chick". *Social Neuroscience*, 5: 309–319; J. Daisley, G. Vallortigara and L. Regolin (2021), "Low-rank *Gallus gallus domesticus* chicks are better at transitive inference reasoning". *Communications Biology*, 4: article no. 1344, doi:10.1038/s42003-021-02855-y.

5 J. Benard and M. Giurfa (2004), "A test of transitive inferences in free-flying honeybees: Unsuccessful performance due to memory constraints". *Learning and Memory*, 11: 328–336.

6 Another explanation could be related to the fact that bees do not have linear hierarchies in their social organisation (foragers all have the same rank). Indeed, Polistes wasps have been shown to solve transitive inference problems instead (E. A. Tibbetts, J. Agudelo, S. Pandit and J. Riocas (2019), "Transitive inference in Polistes paper wasps". *Biology Letters*, published 8 May 2019, doi:10.1098/rsbl.2019.0015. As we have already noted, however, bees and wasps possess very similar miniature brains.

7 M. Siemann and J. Delius (1993), "Implicit deductive responding in humans". *Naturwissenschaften*, 80: 364–366.

8 G. Vallortigara (2018), "L'intelligenza delle galline" [The intelligence of chickens]. *Domenicale del Sole 24 Ore*, 11 February; G. Vallortigara (2017), "Sentience does not require 'higher' cognition. Commentary on Marino on *Thinking Chickens*". *Animal Sentience*, 30(6). G. Vallortigara (2020), "Lessons from miniature brains: Cognition cheap, memory expensive (sentience linked to active movement?)". *Animal Sentience*, 29(17); A. Schnell and G. Vallortigara, (2019), "'Mind' is an ill-defined concept: Considerations for future cephalopod research". *Animal Sentience*, 26(16).

9 S. T. Coleridge (1817), *Biographia Literaria*. Cited in J. L. Borges "The flower of Coleridge". In J. L. Borges ([1952]1968), *Other Inquisitions 1937–1952*. Simon & Schuster, New York.

# 22

# TRACES OF FEELING

A way of documenting experience, i.e. the ability to feel, in creatures that do not possess language was proposed years ago by neuropsychologist Lawrence Weiskrantz.[1] It would be a matter – as in the case of blindsight – of achieving dissociation in responses to the same stimuli, judging them to be absent in an explicit and conscious form, while being able to act on them unconsciously.

A good example is the classic study by neuropsychologists Alan Cowey and Petra Stoerig in which a monkey which had a scotoma (i.e. a blind spot in its field of vision caused by a lesion in the primary visual cortex), had to signal by pressing a button whether or not a bright flash was presented in its healthy visual field.[2] If the flash of light was presented, the monkey had to touch the position corresponding to where the stimulus appeared on the screen; if the flash was not presented, the animal instead had to touch a small square that always remained visible on the screen. In practice, the animal had to classify the stimulus by telling the experimenter – albeit without the use of words – whether the stimulus was there or not.

What happened when the stimulus was presented in the blind spot? As one might expect, the animal classified it as "not there", just as a human being would have classified it.

In a different task (a so-called "reaching" task), the animal simply had to touch the screen at the position where the bright flash had just been shown. Here the monkey was able to respond correctly, whether the stimulus was presented in the healthy field of vision or in the blind spot, thus showing that it saw the stimulus, even though it had "declared" in the previous task that the stimulus *was not there*.

The distinction proposed by the neuropsychologists Melvyn Goodale and David Milner – according to whom the primate brain is equipped with two

DOI: 10.4324/9781003491033-23

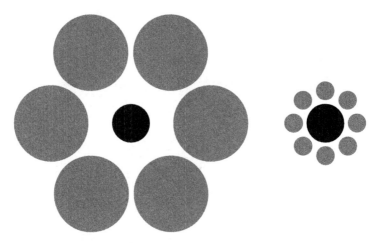

**FIGURE 22.1**    The Ebbinghaus illusion. The two central discs have the same diameter, but appear to be different sizes.

pathways for processing stimuli: a ventral pathway, responsible for the conscious recognition of stimuli, and a dorsal pathway, responsible for the representation of stimuli with a view to action on them, the latter representation being unconscious – has aroused much interest.[3]

A brilliant example of this kind of dissociation was provided by neuropsychologist Salvatore Aglioti with Melvyn Goodale,[4] using one of the most famous and effective optic-geometric illusions, that of Ebbinghaus (Figure 22.1).

As you can see, the central disc surrounded by the larger outer discs looks smaller than the one surrounded by the smaller outer discs. In actual fact, the central discs are identical in size. However, if you ask people to try to grasp the discs by measuring the extension of the pincer movement of the two fingers, you would find, as Aglioti and Goodale observed, that unlike the eye, the fingers of the hand are not fooled, expanding equally at the sight of both central discs, whether surrounded by the smaller or larger discs.

Melvyn Goodale has documented even more spectacular effects.[5] When looking at a cast of a face from the concave side, it is irresistible to see the face as if it were protruding – an illusion first described by the perception psychologist Richard Gregory.[6] However, if people have to try to touch something on the nose of the mask, they direct their hand to the right distance. Once again, the eye is fooled but the hand is not.

What these studies suggest, along with many similar ones conducted on patients with selective dorsal or ventral pathway lesions, is that there are two varieties of seeing: seeing to perceive and seeing to act.

I venture to imagine a possible relationship with the story I have told you so far. First: why does the dorsal pathway not seem to be accompanied by awareness? Perhaps because since an active movement (e.g. that of the hand) is involved, the sensory signal is cancelled in the comparator: the hand moves and goes to meet an object out there, in the world. The object is perceived but the stimulation is not accompanied by a sensation. It is more difficult to understand why stimulation of the ventral pathway instead "feels". The complication stems from the fact that, as Humphrey pointed out, it is not easy for a sensory modality such as sight to be considered in terms of sensation, i.e. as a bodily reaction. However, try to imagine now lying in the sun on a beach and feeling the "touch" of light, what the light does to your body rather than what it tells you about what is out there... A remarkable example of this distinction between feeling and perceiving is provided by Humphrey precisely in reference to touch, tactile stimulation. In sensory substitution experiments, such as the famous one conducted by neuroscientist Paul Bach-y-Rita, blind subjects learn to see thanks to a camera that converts images to a vibration generator transmitted to their skin (e.g. on their back). Each point of skin vibration stimulation corresponds to a small fragment of an image captured by the camera. After training for a few hours, blind people learn to see objects by estimating their distances and sizes. But are they really *seeing* with their skin? As far as perception is concerned, there is no doubt. Objects appear to them as "out there". However, when questioned specifically about the quality of their sensations, about what happens "to them", subjects say they unequivocally experience tactile sensations.[7]

Goodale and Milner's distinction between dorsal and ventral pathways concerns the cortex, but in its more distant origins it essentially involved subcortical structures. The neuroscientist Gerald Schneider[8] was the first, on the basis of a number of classic hamster studies, to argue that the colliculus (a subcortical structure) should serve to locate objects, while structures along the pathway from the thalamus to the cortex should serve to identify objects.

Probably in the primate dorsal pathway, the perception and sensation aspects are now mingled. From the retinas, information is sent to many areas, and so the dorsal/ventral distinction does not fit with the sensation/perception distinction proposed by Reid–Humphrey. Visual agnosias, according to Humphrey, are an example of a situation where sensation is normal but perception is disturbed. In fact, however, things are more complicated because Milner and Goodale studied patients with visual agnosia who, for example, could not tell what the orientation of a slit was, but when asked to put an envelope in it they could do so without difficulty. So they were evidently using perceptual clues of which they were unaware. The fact that they only did this when a direct motor action was required leads me to believe that the efferent copying mechanism was at play. On the other hand, it is not easy to understand (and document) whether and in what way when they simply looked at a slit the sensation of the inclination was accessible to them but not the recognition (perception) of it. This can be guessed, perhaps, by reading what Humphrey says about a case he studied of agnosia for colours.

> The woman patient thought she saw colours as she had always done. When tested for colour blindness with the plates that show a coloured figure against another coloured background, she proved to have normal colour sensitivity, and she could quite well sort coloured discs into same-colour piles. Moreover, when asked "What colour is a banana?' "...a post-box?" and so on, she was right every time. However, when she was shown pieces of coloured paper and asked to say what colour she saw them to be, she made bizarre mistakes: when shown a piece of blue paper – "red"; green paper – "between red and orange"; yellow paper – "blue". Yet, to repeat, she said the quality of her colour vision was quite unaltered – and indeed she was constantly surprised at our taking any interest in this aspect of her case.[9]

How could this help us with creatures from whom we can expect no introspective account of their feelings? Perhaps illusions could be profitable. Not so much to document that animals of other species might be susceptible to the same kind of illusions that we experience: they might in fact be susceptible to illusions in terms of visual behaviour, but without this behaviour being accompanied by consciousness, as is the case with blindsight. Much more advantageous appears to be the circumstance that animals (human and non-human) are not always susceptible to illusions. As far as humans are concerned, an example is the already mentioned case of the Ebbinghaus illusion, which occurs when we look, but not when we grasp. Some indirect evidence would seem to suggest that a similar dissociation is also observed in other species.

The literature on susceptibility to the Ebbinghaus illusion in other animals is very confused.[10] The illusion does not seem to be present in baboons. And it seems to occur in the opposite direction in adult hens and pigeons, which perceive the central disc surrounded by the large outer discs as larger than the one surrounded by the small outer discs. Intrigued by these results, we tried to study the illusion in domestic chicks using a different method, and this time with success: the chicks seem to experience the illusion in the same direction as in humans. The same attempt was made by some colleagues with fish, again successfully.[11] A thousand explanations are possible when different results are obtained by employing different methods in the study of behaviour. However, in this case, one aspect in particular stands out: in the experiments with chickens, pigeons and baboons, the animals were required to perform a manipulative action on the stimulus, pecking for the birds and touching a touch screen for the baboons. With fish and chicks, on the other hand, the motor behaviour did not involve any direct action or manipulation of the stimulus, but more simply, in order to obtain the reward, the animals had to circumvent panels painted on the front with images of the usual discs surrounded by other large or small discs.

One would think that when they act on the stimulus by pecking or touching it, no conscious sensation is involved, because the efferent copy signal – by nullifying the sensory/body reaction – only signals that there is something out there, but nothing that is happening to the animal. For this reason, there would be no illusion either. Illusion, according to my hypothesis, would occur in the realm of "what happens to me" rather than in the realm of "what happens out there". A more prosaic explanation is, of course, to imagine that the two types of action, involving the use of different distances from the stimulus, would make the subjects influenced or not influenced by the context (i.e. whether the inducing discs appear at the extreme periphery of the visual field when approaching to touch or peck). Perhaps. Further experiments are certainly needed. However, the effect of distance seems irrelevant at least in the case of the mask/cast illusion (p. 118): here the viewing distance is fixed, but the hand, unlike the eye, moves at the distance of the cast, while the eye estimates the distance of the protruding face.

There is evidence that in conditioning experiments, animals tend to shape their response according to the nature of the reward. Thus, for example, when trained to peck at a disc to receive a reward, pigeons open their beaks in a different way depending on whether the reward is food or water, as if they were to suck or peck. I would expect chicks, while judging the central discs differently when they have to go around the panels, to open their beaks to the same extent regardless of the size of the surrounding discs when they have to peck at the central discs instead. The existence of such a dissociation could make the hypothesis plausible that it is accompanied by the presence or absence of a feeling.

I would like to underline that the logic behind these arguments, though imperfect, is less imperfect than the traditional argument that because animals *appear sentient to* us then *they must be* sentient (p. 5). Nothing is argued here about the fact that the chicks' behaviour shows a different response to the two central circle stimuli that are objectively equal. Instead, it is observed that, under certain circumstances, the two stimuli induce equal and indistinguishable responses, and these circumstances are those in which the action of an efferent copying mechanism nullifies the sensation aspect but not the perception aspect.

## Notes

1 L. Weiskrantz (1999), *Consciousness Lost and Found: A Neuropsychological Exploration*. Oxford University Press, Oxford.
2 A. Cowey and P. Stoerig (1995), "Blindsight in monkeys". *Nature*, 373: 247–249.
3 M. A. Goodale and A. D. Milner (1992), "Separate visual pathways for perception and action", *Trends in Neuroscience*, 15: 20–25.

4 S. Aglioti, J. F. X. DeSouza and M. A. Goodale (1995), "Size-contrast illusions deceive the eye but not the hand". *Current Biology*, 5: 679–685. See also, for more recent evidence, J. Chen, I. Sperandio and M. A. Goodale (2018), "Proprioceptive distance cues restore perfect size constancy in grasping, but not perception, when vision is limited". *Current Biology*, 28: 927–932. At the time of the translation in English of this book, my old friend Nicola Bruno, a perceptual psychologist of Parma University, makes me aware of some controversies about the original paper on the Ebbinghaus illusion, see K. K. Kopiske, N. Bruno, C. Hesse, T. Schenk and V. H. Franz (2016), "The functional subdivision of the visual brain: Is there a real illusion effect on action? A multi-lab replication study". *Cortex*, 79: 130–152 and the reply of the original authors in the same journal. Let's see: science is an auto-corrective process. Nonetheless the clinical evidence for a ventral pathway, responsible for a conscious recognition of stimuli, and a dorsal pathway, responsible for an unconscious representation of stimuli, looks convincing and tenable.

5 G. Kroliczak, P. Heard, M. A. Goodale and R. L. Gregory (2006), "Dissociation of perception and action unmasked by the hollow-face illusion", *Brain Research*, 1080, 9–16.

6 R. Gregory (1970), *The Intelligent Eye*. Weidenfeld and Nicolson, London.

7 P. P. Bach-y-Rita (1972), *Brain Mechanisms in Sensory Substitution*. Academic Press, New York/London.

8 G. E. Schneider (1967), "Contrasting visuomotor functions of tectum and cortex in the golden hamster". *Psychologische Forschung*, 31, 52–62.

9 J. M. Oxbury, S. M. Oxbury and N. Humphrey (1969), "Varieties of colour anomia". *Brain*, 92(4), 847–860.

10 C. Parron, and J. Fagot (2007), "Comparison of grouping abilities in humans (*Homo sapiens*) and baboons (*Papio papio*) with Ebbinghaus illusion". *Journal of Comparative Psychology*, 121: 405–411; N. Nakamura, S. Watanabe and K. Fujita (2008), "Pigeons perceive the Ebbinghaus-Titchener circles as an assimilation illusion". *Journal of Experimental Psychology: Animal Behavior Processes*, 34: 375–387; N. Nakamura, S. Watanabe and K. Fujita (2014), "A reversed Ebbinghaus-Titchener illusion in bantams (*Gallus gallus domesticus*)". *Animal Cognition*, 17: 471– 481.

11 O. Rosa-Salva, R. Rugani, A. Cavazzana, L. Regolin and G. Vallortigara (2013), "Perception of the Ebbinghaus illusion in four-day-old domestic chicks (*Gallus gallus*)". *Animal Cognition*, 16: 895–906; V. A. Sovrano, L. Albertazzi and O. Rosa-Salva (2015), "The Ebbinghaus illusion in a fish (*Xenotoca eiseni*)". *Animal Cognition*, 18: 533–542. For a review on this kind of study see also: O. Rosa-Salva, V. A. Sovrano and G. Vallortigara (2014), "What can fish brains tell us about visual perception?". *Frontiers in Neural Circuits*, 8: 119; G. Vallortigara (2006), "The cognitive chicken: Visual and spatial cognition in a non-mammalian brain". In *Comparative Cognition: Experimental Explorations of Animal Intelligence*, E. A. Wasserman and T. R. Zentall, (eds.), pp. 41–58, Oxford University Press, Oxford. T. Matsushima, E.-I.Izawa, N. Aoki, and S. Yanagihara (2003), "The mind through chick eyes: Memory, cognition and anticipation". *Zoological Sciences*, 20(4): 395–408.

# 23

## AND SO...

Doodle-bug, doodle-bug,
tell me what I want to know.[1]

As a child, at mass, the recitation of the Nicaea-Constantinople Creed filled
me with a perplexing sensation. I did not quite understand the source of the
convictions I had to enunciate in a loud, ringing voice, but at the same time
I sensed their power.

*I believe in one God,*
*Almighty Father,*
*Creator of Heaven and Earth,*
*of all things visible and invisible.*

Having left the years of certainty behind me, I am now disenchantedly
permitted to enunciate only beliefs of imperfect content and precarious duration. My provisional beliefs about the visible and invisible things mentioned
in this book boil down to more or less this.

It seems to me the conjecture is tenable that the essential forms of thought,
as manifested in the inferential operations that can be conducted about the
location in space and time of the objects, numerable or not, that populate
our phenomenal world, and about the causes of their behaviour, is the same
in all animal organisms, at least in its immediate and implicit manifestation.[2] Indeed, I observe that the essential forms of thought are manifested in
creatures endowed with miniaturised brains, and I therefore deduce that the
computational operations that support them must be relatively simple and
require only a modest number of nerve cells.

DOI: 10.4324/9781003491033-24

The calculation strategies, the original stratagems that have been devised in the course of evolution to extract and classify information, seem to have been around since the dawn of the constitution of brains. And subsequent improvements seem to have been more in quantity than quality: more capable memories, parallel computing strategies...

The most remarkable finding, the birth of experience – consciousness – manifests itself for the first time, I believe, with the need for the organism to distinguish between the self-generated stimulation of its own activity from that which it receives from the rest of the world (whatever that is) outside. This brings into effect the minimum conditions for experience: an inner actively defining itself against an outer. I therefore think, along with many others, that the feedforward circuit of the efferent copy played a key role in the emergence of conscious sensation, that it was in particular the basis for the distinction between the two provinces, first hypothesised by Thomas Reid, which creatures actively moving in the world inhabit: that of feeling and that of perceiving.

I can already hear Professor Christof Koch's voice here, commenting "Of course this was necessary, but not sufficient..." (p. 62). The fact is, however, that there are various kinds of necessity, each more or less close to the core of experience. A beating heart, a cortico-thalamic system, the excitability of neurons, calcium channels... These may all be necessary, but they do not qualify the necessity of the appearance of experience, as does the idea that there is a system that compares the feedforward signal of the bodily response with the incoming sensory signal in order to distinguish, for the first time in the history of life on Earth, what happens to me from what happens out there.

I do not find plausible the idea – despite its popularity among my colleagues – that consciousness should mysteriously emerge once the nervous system has reached a certain degree of complexity. If this were the case, we should be able to observe, at least in the members of our species, that the inability to conduct complex cognitive activities goes hand in hand with the loss of the capacity to be sentient, which is patently false. The phenomena of blindsight, as we have noted, occur not only in the perceptual realm but also in the cognitive realm. It is possible for humans to draw sophisticated logical inferences in the absence of awareness of their execution, both in form and content. I therefore welcome the conjecture (admittedly, as yet *unproven*) that the mere computations carried out by a few damp and humble cells constitute a plausible substrate of consciousness, in its essential manifestation: the capacity to feel, to have experiences.

### Notes

1 The nursery rhyme about the doodle-bug is part of American folklore. Mark Twain included it in his *Adventures of Tom Sawyer* (1876).
2 I say its immediate and implicit manifestation because I am convinced that language, with its possibility of making the contents of thought operations explicit

and socially shareable, has changed the possibilities of use (even if not the mechanics) of mental processes in our species by to a fair degree. But this is another discussion, which I have already made elsewhere (see pp. 126–134 in G. Vallortigara (2008), *Cervello di gallina. Visite guidate tra etologia e neuroscienze* [Chicken brain. Guided tours between ethology and neuroscience]. Bollati-Boringhieri, Turin. To understand what is special about human language see A. Moro (2017), *Le lingue impossibili* [Impossible languages]. Cortina, Milan; A. Moro (2019), *La razza e la lingua* [Race and language]. La Nave di Teseo, Milan.

# AUTHOR INDEX

# SUBJECT INDEX

3 - cognitive feat of bees
6 - 'neurological surplus' for memory
11 - conditioning in an ant lion larva
12 - beetle adults remember larval learning

Printed in Great Britain
by Amazon